PRINCIPLES OF A SUCCESSFUL
Entrepreneur

Sheldon Razin

Edition 1.0

Principles of a Successful Entrepreneur

by Sheldon Razin
Edition 1.0

ISBN: 978-0-692-28953-2

This book is dedicated to Graeme Frehner,
my business partner and best friend

Contents

Contents continued

Chapter 1

WHY LISTEN TO ME?

Because I was you

I started my software company forty years ago with $2,000 and built it into a multi-billion-dollar value with no debt and no venture money.

That's right: we never had any debt; we never had any venture money.

Not many people have done that, but if I were to start all over today, I could do it again. I want to tell you how I did it, and how you can, too.

Some people have asked me, "Can you teach entrepreneurism? Can you tell me how to be a Steve Jobs?"

The answer is no, I can't teach you to be a Steve Jobs. He was one in a million. But I can tell you how to be pretty good. The superstar component is something you're born with. There were too many elements of his inner soul, too many factors that he inherited in his genes and were fostered by his early environment. I can't replicate them. But I can make you a better entrepreneur, because, frankly, if I could do it, anyone who really wants to can do it.

I was a very unlikely entrepreneur. Why was I unlikely? My educational background. I went to college and graduated in mathematics. I never had a course in business, never had a course in economics. Nothing associated with business at all. Zero. From 1955 to 1959. The courses were available; I never took them.

Even though I never prepared myself to build a company, something in my blood always wanted to be an entrepreneur. I wanted to control my own life, to beat the odds, to be the go-to guy who figured things out—and make some money in the process. When I was just thirteen, I jumped over the fence at Wonderland Greyhound Park in Revere, Massachusetts, about five miles outside of downtown Boston, and tried to beat the dog races. My compatriots and I cobbled together a $2 bet, and I was the mathematician who figured out how the dogs were going to run around the track. I graduated to horse racing before I went to college.

Figure it out, make some money.

Fortunately, I was born with an analytical ability, an innate gift of analysis, which I honed at Massachusetts Institute of Technology (MIT). I analyzed every experience I went through, looking for what lessons I could learn from it to make me better.

Everyone has innate gifts, aspects of their personality or unique thought processing. The trick is to recognize your own gift(s) and then hone and incorporate them into your regular dealings. It starts with an intense self-awareness.

When I looked at the individual experiences I went through, I never blamed anybody for bad outcomes, because I knew I wouldn't learn anything that way. Saying, "Well, the reason things went bad is because so and so did this wrong thing" wouldn't get me anywhere and left no room for personal growth. What I'd say to myself was, "What did *I* do wrong?" Or, "What could *I* have done better?"

It's never about what *someone else* could or should have done. It's always about *you*, the entrepreneur—the one in charge, the one who has to come up with the answers, the one who has to figure out what to do next. You're the one who needs to learn the lessons, so you can overcome your own weaknesses.

When you do something about a weakness you have, all of a sudden you're stronger than anyone else. That's growth.

To My Reader

A lot of the lessons in this book are of value to people who aren't in business. They're of value to people in general.

Somewhere in here are principles of negotiation. You negotiate all the time with everybody: with your wife, with your children. Negotiations occur regularly in everyday life.

You might have goals that have nothing to do with business but that require perseverance and innovation. You need some good luck; you need the absence of bad luck.

The analytical methodology can make things better. You went through an experience and it didn't turn out right: what can you learn from it? That's universal.

The ability to say you're wrong is important in all aspects of life. In fact, it is life.

No one is good at everything. I was always very leery of my own memory, so years ago I started recording everything I did during the day in a notebook. If I met someone, I'd record the date, the person's name, what we talked about. As a result, I had a better memory than people with good memories. Don't let what you don't know or can't do stop you.

This is life.

One last note: I founded Quality Systems, Inc., or QSI, in 1973 and took it public in 1982. I was either the sole proprietor or CEO for most of the company's history. After I retired from my position as CEO, I continued to lead QSI as its founder and Independent Chairman of the Board of Directors, and I still take great pride in helping its board and management team.

The stories, lessons, philosophies, and beliefs I share in this book, however, were not written on behalf of the company. They're from my nearly half a century of entrepreneurial and business success. I hope they will provide some guidance for you as you travel your own road to entrepreneurial success.

Chapter 2

NOT ALL GREAT IDEAS WORK OUT

I honed my analytic skills at MIT

MIT always published the test questions from the prior three years' core classes—math, physics, and chemistry—to give people an idea of what their upcoming quizzes would be like. Anyone could pick up a copy of the questions at the bulletin board.

The fraternities at MIT always had super-smart people who would ace the quizzes and then save their returned tests in a file at the fraternity house. Their members not only had access to the questions but also to the correct answers.

I wasn't in a fraternity. I was a member of the 5:15 Club, an organization for commuters. When I realized that I and many of my fellow students didn't have access to those fraternity files, I saw an opportunity. "How can I bring this to the rest of the student body—or even do a *better* job than the fraternity people?"

I wanted to not just provide the answers to the quizzes; I wanted to explain how to arrive at the answers.

As a senior, I was Freshman Advisor to a very bright student whose last name was Feldman. I took him aside and said, "Why don't you do the chemistry, I'll do the math, and we'll split up the physics. We won't just answer the questions; we'll write the solutions in such a way that they're almost a course by itself."

This was my first experience in giving added value. The frat guys were giving their people the right answers. I wanted my pamphlets to also provide the thought process of how to get to those right answers. I thought, "We'll do it at MIT, and then we'll take it across the nation. I know how to do this: you get a few bright guys and they do all the tests." I still wasn't interested in business, but this seemed like an easy way to make some extra money.

Feldman agreed, so the two of us went to work. MIT let me use their mimeograph machine for free, but typing it up was a mess because typewriters didn't have mathematical symbols in those days. We had to write in certain equations and symbols. I did some of it, and a friend's mother ended up typing up some of it. Then we had to collate the whole thing.

My extended family used to come to our house every Sunday from Brockton and Haverhill, so one Sunday I set up an assembly line to put the pages together. We all went around the table gathering mimeographed pages into packages. Then we stapled them into booklets with front and back card-stock covers.

The original idea was to sell them off street corners, but I looked across the street from 77 Mass Avenue, where MIT is, and saw the Technology Bookstore and thought of another opportunity. "Instead of selling onesies, why don't we sell the whole thing to the Technology Bookstore?"

I showed the booklets to the store manager. "Do you think these things will sell?"

He said, "They'll sell like hotcakes."

"Good! Then you'll take the whole lot."

He said, "Not so fast."

"What do you mean, 'not so fast'?"

"We're owned by the Institute. We can't do this unless we get permission. Do you mind giving me a copy of your stuff?"

About a week later I got a call from the Dean's office. As I walked into his office, he started reciting: "You're Sheldon Razin. You were born on this day; you're taking these classes...." He knew everything about me.

He said, "Would you like to graduate?"

"What do you mean? Oh, I see you have one of my books. What did you do with them?"

"I gave them all to the department heads."

"What did they think of them?"

"They thought they were too good."

"What do you mean, 'too good'?"

"The department heads think that with your book, students won't have to take the course. They can just use your documents. So we don't want you to sell them. In fact, if you want to graduate, don't sell them."

It was a blow, but it was also a lesson: don't try to compete with your own organization. I had the whole blueprint, but I had taken it to the wrong customer. I should have stuck with selling the booklets one at a time, or talked to a publisher about creating a series of study guides.

Instead, I graduated and moved on.

Chapter 3

SELL WHAT YOU HAVE, EVEN IF IT'S ONLY YOURSELF

No loans, no venture capital—
just two guys with a lot of moxie.

I spent about a decade working for other people before I couldn't take it anymore. By the time I decided to go out on my own, I was a software manager at the Autonetics division of North American Aviation, which later became Rockwell and then Boeing. I knew a lot about writing software, I knew a good deal about working with people, and I was friends with a lot of people in my field.

I also had a wife, two kids, and a mortgage on a home in Corona, California.

And $2,000.

I set up Quality Systems in a back room of my house. I was a sole proprietor, which meant I was solely responsible for everything. I started the business by cold calling want ads to sell myself as a consultant in place of a new hire. I figured it was a win-win situation: the client would get what he needed without the cost of employee benefits or Human Resources management, and I'd get the funds to grow my company.

There were times when I felt like a hooker or a prostitute. I was selling my brain for money.

At that time, Bourns, an electronic component company, was using optical mark recognition (OMR) to create data files for major telephone companies. Bourns had contracts with AT&T and Southwest Bell, as well as many other companies, but they had a big problem: the things they were trying to design didn't work.

When I called on the ad, I reached John Vogelpol, the manager for software development. He already knew me and my abilities because he used to work for me at Rockwell, so I asked what he needed.

He said his group of some twenty or more people had been working on a problem for a year or two, but they were no closer to completing the project than they had been on Day One.

I said, "John, let me take a look at it."

I took Graeme Frehner, my friend and technology genius, with me to see what the team had been doing for two years. We both immediately realized it was technically unsound because certain fundamentals in the design were impossible. No matter how much longer the team labored, the system they were trying to create wouldn't work.

John gave us the go-ahead, and the two of us scrapped everything the others had done, started over from scratch, and finished the job inside a couple of months.

And it worked.

John and his boss, Oscar Olsen, were ecstatic. Not only had we delivered the product, we'd done it in less than three months. His reaction was exactly what we hoped for. He pulled out a laundry list of projects and said, "Gee, can you do *this* for me? And this? And this?"

We had no offices, no company structure, and no products, but we each did 2,880 billable hours that first year. It not only funded the company, it put food on both our families' tables and convinced me I'd made the right move.

Chapter 4

CHOOSE YOUR CUSTOMERS WISELY

Part I

"This second year," I told Graeme, "we're going to take half of what we make from selling our brain power and use it to start developing our own products."

We were still working out of my back room, which is not uncommon for new businesses. Many of the "superstars," like Steve Jobs and Larry Ellison, started in their garages. And, like many others, we quickly got to the point where we needed to look bigger or more impressive than we possibly could working out of the house.

Since this was the era when technology was segueing from mainframes to minicomputers, I teamed up with Media III, a minicomputer manufacturer. Customers would say, "Where's your office?" and I'd meet them in one of Media III's empty rooms. It was an impressive building, and the customer assumed it was mine.

We all did that: Ellison, Jobs, me, everyone. We all started with nothing, we all had to impress some people, so we all fudged a little bit about how big we were, how good we were, in order to get started. Putting on a show at someone else's facility is a lot smarter than leasing office space before you have the revenue, profits, and cash flow to sustain the move. In our case, it kept us from making the wrong move at a crucial time in our growth.

Eventually, I wanted my own office space, so I went to look at a place for rent in my hometown, Corona. The owner's office was located next to a bowling alley, which he also owned. I didn't know anything about bowling, but as I was waiting for the owner to show up, I noticed people working out computations by hand.

I asked, "What are you doing?"

When they said they were calculating bowling handicaps, it dawned on me that here was another opportunity. Computers could do their computations faster, easier, and better. "I can deliver what they need far more cost-effectively than they can."

We didn't end up renting that guy's building. Instead, we leased an office in Tustin at what was then called the Meredith Financial Center on 17th Street and Prospect. But in the course of our search, I came to understand a little more about bowling because a friend's girlfriend bowled in a league. Graeme and I created a product we could sell to the leagues themselves, because there were hundreds of leagues. We had to invest in all the necessary forms and papers, which was quite an expense for a young, two-person startup.

After months of trying to sell our system to the leagues, we realized the product was generating all of sixteen dollars a week.

"This is 'Razin's Folly,'" Graeme quipped. "You've blown it."

Now, for me that was a challenge. I'd wake up in the middle of the night, thinking about how to turn this situation around. One night, Eureka! I called Graeme.

"I've got it."

"You've got what?"

"I know how to sell this system. I know how to make it into a great business."

By then I knew various people who computed these league and recap sheets: Doris Rudell, an ex-professional bowler; Jean Evans, and one or two others. I knew our software could do their job far more effectively than they could, but they already had the customers. They didn't have to pitch to the leagues; the leagues were already signed on for their services.

I told Graeme, "I'm going to call each one of these people up, invite them to a seminar, and show them how we can process these league handicap sheets faster and easier as a timeshare, at $xx per hour."

They all came to the seminar, but they all said "No, no, no" to the timeshare.

"We get paid $x per bowler, so we want to pay you $y per bowler."

That's the way they ran their business.

I said, "Okay," reflected on the difference between their rigid stance and my flexibility, and changed my model to $.04 a bowler.

Then they wanted to make sure I wouldn't compete with them; I wouldn't try to sell my product directly to the leagues themselves. I already wasn't making any money doing that, so I said, "I promise I will not sell directly to any leagues at all. I'll only sell through you. I will not be a competitor of yours."

"Will you put that in writing?"

"Absolutely. I demand only one thing. Once a week, you pay me for my services. If you don't, I'm going to stop processing—and, parenthetically, you'll be out of business."

One hundred percent of those people signed up to use my per-bowler service. The program itself only took a fraction of our computer power. It ran in the background while other programs were running, so it didn't cost anything extra to process these sheets.

We immediately started making an actual profit. The program was so low-key, I could hire a college student to come in at night just to keep an eye on the printer and fix any paper jams. "You can do your homework, you can write your papers, you can weave rugs for all I care. Just make sure the forms keep printing."

That business grew to be a cash cow, a total money-making machine. Graeme, a technical genius, put up a program that showed how much we were producing and making in real time. It was like watching a slot machine rack up one win after another or a steady drip fill up a bucket—except the drip was money, not water, and the bucket was our bank account. I could go online any time, day or night, to see the figures grow moment by moment.

That was a big thrill!

At one point, I told my collective customers: "By the way, I've looked at your costs. You'd be far better off paying me on a timeshare basis."

"Nope," they all said. "We want to keep paying $.04 a bowler."

How could I not grin? "If that's what you want, you've got it."

In the end, we were the leading provider for computing bowling handicaps in Southern California. We used up all those forms I had bought and stored in my attic and many, many more. That one product generated $100,000 of literally pure profit every year—and those were 1970 dollars. Today, the figure would be closer to $600,000.

Part II

So we had a bowling-league product that was successful. We had a word processor, which was a horizontal market. We'd developed a portfolio performance-measurement data-entry system for A.G. Becker Securities in Chicago, a brokerage firm. We had another product we'd created for Reliable Auto, an auto parts company, an inventory system for Bourns, and a time-share system for dentists.

So we had all these systems, all these products, and we only had six people in the company. It was crazy. I'd tell people, "We'll work for you, you can have unlimited license, but I own the software." That was a condition. Every time Quality Systems (QSI) did a project, I owned it. The customer had unlimited use forever, but I owned the rights to the software.

This was crucial; ownership is the secret to the software or any other business. You write software for a customer, but you own it. Then you can sell it over and over again. It's like writing a book once, then selling as many copies as you can. It's the same principle in any business. The ability to keep selling the same product, with or without improvements over time, is one of the elements that separates entrepreneurs from freelancers whose intellectual property is owned by the person or company that hires them. Ownership is absolutely crucial to sustaining and growing any company.

With a business model like that, we needed clarity for our array of business prospects, which included bowlers, brokerage firms, auto parts, and dentists. We had more opportunity than the six of us could handle. We sat around a table and asked, "What are we going to do?" We looked at each of these businesses. We had bowlers, but that wasn't something I really wanted to do, not a clientele I wanted to pursue. The brokerage thing was a one-of-a-kind product we had done for A.G. Becker Securities. The auto-parts inventory thing was a possibility, but I wasn't really enthusiastic about it.

Ah, but dentists: they were a clientele I could relate to. We had a timeshare system for dentists, for which we hired a salesman. His greatest contribution was that he never sold anything, because timeshare was the wrong thing for dentists at that time. So we developed a turnkey system that could be installed in the dental office. It had a great payback: a dentist could recoup the cost of the whole system in a year. From then on, the system just made them money through savings and added revenue.

I was more comfortable with dentists than bowlers or auto-parts dealers. They were educated, they were professionals, and they felt like a more definable, consistent, and refined segment of society that had a need we could solve and the economic standing to pay us.

That's how we chose our product and our target client. We immediately went national with the product. We quickly discovered that group practices would benefit from our automation processes far more than a solo dentist could. That gave us our product focus and our ideal client profile. From there, we merely had to grow and expand.

Chapter 5

ALL BUSINESS IS JUST THREE THINGS

It has to be good for the customer. It has to be good for the employees. And it has to be good for the shareholders. In our company, we took these basic realities one step further: it not only had to be good, it had to be unsurpassed.

1) It Has to Be Good for the Customer

The customer is better off buying your service or product than doing nothing, <u>and</u> he's better off buying it from you than from a competitor.

From the beginning, Graeme and I shared one guiding philosophy: to be the best at anything we did. We didn't want to put out any product that was just "okay." We wanted everything we did to be the best—and not just the best in Southern California or the U.S. or North America. We wanted it to be the best in the world.

Any prospective employee who didn't have that philosophy just didn't fit in. Quality Systems developed only world-class products—and our insistence on that paid off immediately. Multi-national customers like the Saudi Arabian Oil Company, also known as Saudi Aramco or just Aramco, came from Saudi Arabia unsolicited to buy our system. Why? Because what we produced was unsurpassed in the marketplace, and people recognized our products as the best.

That was another shared philosophy: we wanted the people who used our products to be the ones who labeled us the best. When we produced that A+ product for Bourns in less than three months at a fraction of the cost for their people to keep working on it, we created a win-win situation, which is a basic component of making it "good for the customer." If it's good for the customer, it's going to be good for us, too, because not only will we get paid, but word of our excellence will spread to others who want the best.

2) It Has to Be Good for the Employees

The employee is better off working for you than working for anyone else.

Anyone who shares the philosophy of being the best rightly has an expectation of being treated the same way: as the best, in the best manner possible, with the best opportunities, the best challenges, and the best total compensation, which include stock options or other forms of equity compensation. Otherwise, why would they give their best?

For example, we hired Carl Yilunto at ePace!, another company I financed, for $100,000 per year plus options. After he worked for us for about three years, he cashed out at $1,135,000 at capital gains tax rates. That's taking care of your employees!

As with our dedication to excellence, this circular ideology has produced remarkable dividends for our employees and enterprises— another win-win that defines our corporate success. We encourage people to be not just as good as they think they can be, but even more than they ever thought possible. We don't push them past their limits; we just try to help them stretch those limits.

We've found that people who are dedicated to excellence respond to challenge with eagerness, even when they're not quite sure they're up to the dare.

Along those same lines, there is no mindless drudgery at Quality Systems. Everyone's job is important and integral to the whole, and they know it. It's one way we show respect to every single employee.

Part of my respect comes from knowing exactly what each activity entails. I purposely did every job in the company, from data entry to secretarial—I typed, I used my word processor; I even brought people coffee—to client management, to training, to software development, to sales. I did everything. If a mess needed cleaning up or the floor swept before a customer came in, I did it.

That was crucial for me as a human being and to my success. I didn't feel I understood every job, couldn't put myself in my employees' place, unless I did it.

Another way was our first-name, open-door policy at all levels. Anyone could talk to anyone at Quality Systems. No one had to send a complaint or suggestion or concern "up through the channels." If someone had a problem, they could email me, call me, stop me in the hallway, knock on my door, or set up an appointment to see me. And I had a principle: if you called me, I'd get back to you within 24 hours. Your call didn't go into a black hole.

I started a practice in the early days of the company of giving everyone a little gift on the day of our annual Christmas party. One time it was a pen, another time a clock. We'd wrap them all, and I personally handed it to every single individual who worked for me. At the beginning, I started my deliveries at 10:00 a.m. and finished at noon because we were a small company. As we grew, I began at 7:00 a.m. and finished at 4:30 p.m. I'd leave off just in time to go to our party. It was a wonderful learning experience because I talked with everyone.

"Hey, you're in field service. Are we having any problems with any of our products?"

"Oh, yeah, we're having a lot of problems with our printers."

"What printers? What problems?"

I found out about the kinds of things that wouldn't show up in a report, the day-to-day functions of this department and that employee. Eventually, the company got so big that I didn't know everybody by their first name, so somebody had to give me a prep list as I went into each department area.

"These are the people you're going to meet in the next five minutes. These are their names; this is who they are and what they do...."

That kind of personal contact with, and interest in, every employee not only demonstrates respect and support, it creates an environment of camaraderie, loyalty, and *esprit de corps*. Overlay that with our philosophy of challenge and encouragement—and, of course, the best compensation packages possible—and you have another win-win, another layer of "good for" that contributes to our overall success.

3) It Has to Be Good for the Shareholders

The company is making money and growing.

It goes without saying that a company has to make money to stay in business. To keep its customers serviced, its employees happy, and its shareholders satisfied, the company also has to do more than just break even. It has to grow every year in revenue, profit, and cash flow, or what I call the Adjusted Flow: revenue earned as the result of company effort. You don't get credit for cash borrowed from a bank or contributed by an investor.

This circular philosophy of excellence creates a win-win for those people and entities who invest their money and confidence in the company. The paradigm of employees giving their peak performance to deliver world-class products and service to highly satisfied customers has no choice but to generate exponential growth, thus making it "good for the stockholders."

- Peak performance

- World-class products

- Highly satisfied customers

These three principles have been true for thousands of years in every industry and for every kind of business, from large corporations to one-man shops. They're the principles of good business, period.

Chapter 6

THREE BOTTOM LINES

Revenue, Profit, and Cash Flow

When I worked at Rockwell, I knew a brilliant man named Sy Rubenstein. Sometimes I worked for him; sometimes he worked for me. At one point, our career paths diverged. I opened my own business, while he climbed the ladder all the way up to become the head of Rockwell's space-shuttle program.

In his later years, Sy came to work at QSI, but my experience of negotiating with him taught me a tremendous lesson. Every time I tried to hire him, he wanted guarantees I couldn't meet.

He said, "I need your promise of this, this, and this, or I can't make a move."

I said, "I can't guarantee that. I have no guarantees, so I can't offer any to you."

We finally signed a contract, but then we started talking about how we were going to measure him. That's when I realized how paramount those three measures of a company are. Bottom line: the formula for measuring any company's success or lack thereof is simply Revenues, Profits, and Cash Flow.

You need to have all three. You can jimmy any two or three to look good, but you can't run a healthy business unless they're all good. If revenues are growing, profit should be growing and so should cash. If they're not, something is wrong.

Suppose you have a business where your revenue is growing because you're selling an automobile well below cost, say for $1,000. Your revenues may go off the charts, but you're not making any profit and you have no cash flow; in other words, you're in trouble.

Another instance: your sales are good and you make a good profit on every deal, but your customers aren't paying you on time. That leaves you with no cash flow; you have nothing in the bank to keep the company solvent. Two out of three still isn't good enough.

If you measure all three elements simultaneously—revenue, profit, and cash flow—you cannot jimmy the system without committing fraud, and you cannot fool yourself into thinking you're running a healthy business when you're really not.

Chapter 7

SEE IT FIRST, SEE IT BEST

An entrepreneur needs the ability to picture the future before anyone else does. They have to see it.

I am reminded of Ted Williams, one of the greatest baseball players of all time and the last ballplayer to bat over .400 in a single season.

Williams' eyesight was 20/10, twice as good as normal vision. His vision was so legendary that rumor had it umpires wouldn't call any pitch a strike unless he swung at it because he wouldn't swing if it wasn't over the plate.

Not only could he always see if a pitch was in the strike zone, he could see the rotation on the ball.

That's vision. He could see something that people with normal vision couldn't.

An entrepreneur needs that same kind of foresight, that same ability to see what others don't. The superstar entrepreneurs—Steve Jobs (Apple), Mark Zuckerberg (Facebook), Larry Page (Google), Evan Williams (Twitter), et al—all had it, and they used their 20/10 vision to change the world.

Jobs alone transformed three industries. He reinvented the music industry with the iPod, making CD players obsolete almost overnight. He completely upgraded the mobile phone business with his iPhone. Before Apple released their easiest-to-use cell phone, the industry was dominated by Motorola, Nokia, Nextel, all famous names that suddenly found their market shares floundering. Jobs used new technology to essentially wipe the competition from the board.

Then he came out with the iPad, a PC and laptop killer. I used to go on a plane with a laptop under my seat. Now I carry a small, thin device that weighs nothing and is faster and has more power than any PC or laptop I ever had.

Jobs transformed three industries because he could see the future. He visualized how solid-state memory devices with no moving parts would revolutionize business, and said, "I can do that!" He saw how everything would evolve, and he saw it before anyone else.

Larry Page saw the array of Internet search engines—some with limited database access, others that insisted on fees—and simplified Web searches into a new, single verb. "Hang on, let me Google that." Yes, there are still dozens of other Internet search engines; they compete for the slim 30-35 percent of the market that Google *doesn't* control.

Williams' 140-character Twitter platform, unimaginable before the 21st century, is so ever-present and powerful, it has launched a new version of the English language, leveled the playing field between those in power and those who put them into power, and impacted the political, social, and economic landscape in the most remote areas of the globe.

What they all did was see what certain technology *could do* to transform an industry. That's their insight. Other people saw the same technology, but not that, "If I put this together with that and the other thing, I'll have…." whatever it was: an iPad, a search engine, or social network—some so ubiquitous their very names have entered our lexicon. "Did you Google that?" "His tweet went viral."

The technology was there for everyone to see, but only those with the vision realized how to use those components to create revolutionary products and services. That's vision; that's seeing potential and possibilities no one else saw, and either acting on them before anyone else could, or doing them better than anyone else.

The combination of being first and being the best is almost unbeatable in any business.

Chapter 8

PARTNER UP

*Ted Williams may have stood in the batter's box by himself,
but the people who transform the world have help.*

Jobs and Gates and all the others, including me, not only saw the
various technology parts and pieces and had the insight to know what
they could do with it, they also had a partner (or two) who knew how
to create the technology we needed.

Steve Jobs and Bill Gates could *see what to do* with the
components Steve Wozniak and Paul Allen created. Wozniak
and Allen had the technological *genius*; Jobs and Gates had the
technological vision. That's the kind of partnership a company needs:
someone who invents, someone who knows *what they can do* with
those inventions.

I had Graeme Frehner. One day he came into my office to show me something he'd done on the computer. This was the era of the minicomputer, remember, which was connected to and run by individual workstations. At the end of the day, everyone turned off their terminal and went home. The computer power was vacant until the first person came in the next morning at 7:30 or 8:00 a.m. Nothing ran at night.

Graeme said, "Watch what I can do. I created a new function that allows us to run tasks at a later time when no one is using or monitoring the machines. It can even tell another terminal to go do a task. What do you think?"

What did I think? I jumped up and down with excitement! I stood on a chair. I said, "Graeme! Do you realize what you've invented?"

He said, "It's just a little technical thing."

"It's just a little technical thing that can make computers work twenty-four hours a day!"

That was his invention, something that had never been done before. We labeled it the Overnight Processor. I couldn't have done it without him, but he couldn't see its value without me.

A lot of people said, "It's just a little thing; nobody's going to buy it. You should just give it away."

I said, "No, we can charge for it. They'll buy it."

And they did. We sold it to 100 percent of our client base. Not 95 percent, not 98 percent. One hundred percent. That certainly made it buyable.

That took both sides of the partnership: Graeme's ability to see and create this phenomenal component and my set of skills to say, "Wow! With this I can make computers work all night long on anything I want them to do!"

Concentrated vision, large-scale vision.

Genius and Visionary

You may wonder why it takes both partners to build a company. I remember once when Graeme and I had grown our business enough to be making decent money, and he asked me, "Why do we have to make a big company? I like what we're doing."

I was the one who wanted to not just be the best, but to make a mark in the world. I was the one with the drive and the vision. I told him, "Graeme, we can grow this into something really, really special."

It's the entrepreneur, not the technological genius or guru, who brings the vision and drive to the table. It's the entrepreneur who says, "I'm going to do this; I'm going to grow this as big as I can make it."

It takes both sides, both sets of skills to make it happen, the tech guru and the business visionary. Gates had Paul Allen. Jobs had Steve Wozniak. I had Graeme Frehner.

Who do you have?

Chapter 9

CREATIVE INNOVATION

An entrepreneur should be able to whip together an answer on the spur of the moment.

That ability requires amassing as much information as possible beforehand. When I pitch to a potential client, for example, I learn everything I can about him first. I want to know about his practice, his character, everything I can find out about his needs, who he is, and why he might be buying now. All that information lets me know how I can help him.

I had a key salesman named Grant Sadler. Grant found out that Morris Cohen, the owner of a dental group in Northern California, was coming down to Orange County to buy a competitor's system.

"Can you get me in front of him?" I asked Grant.

"He says the only time he has is at Orange County airport."

"Okay, I'll meet him there."

I learned that Cohen was using a manual billing system and currently had a set of unbilled insurance receivables around $100,000. For whatever reason, he was unable to bill for all that insurance money.

I knew I had a data-conversion/data-entry department that was unique in the industry. No one else in the dental industry was doing data conversion, which amounted to inputting the information from the customer's handwritten or typed ledger cards into the computer to create a database. Our conversion department not only did that for our customers, it also had the ability to convert the data from certain competitors' systems into ours.

When I heard about Cohen's unbilled insurance, I immediately saw an opportunity. I already had the department; why not use all that data-entry talent for something new, something more? We could easily convert Cohen's handwritten bills into digital records and send them out to the insurance companies by computer.

That was the leap; that was the innovation. No other company offered insurance-billing conversion at the time—including the one whose system Cohen had already decided to buy. I saw what no one else saw, I saw it first, and I saw how I could close the sale with an offer no one else could make.

I caught up with Morris Cohen at the airport and said, "Look, I know you're ready to buy, but I also know my product is better—it's the best, in fact—and not only will it give you the best results, but I won't offer you a deal I wouldn't take myself."

He said, "I'm listening."

I said, "What if I could bill all your outstanding insurance in one month so you collect your full $100,000 account receivables? That revenue alone will more than pay for the entire system."

"Will you put that in writing?" he asked.

"Everything I tell you I'll put in writing."

It was an impossible-to-refuse proposition, and I created it on the spot, out of thin air. That's innovation. That's seeing the components that are already there and realizing what else could be done with them. He was ready to buy, he had already made up his mind to go with a competitor's product, and yet I showed up *at the airport* with a capability he couldn't get anywhere else—because we only create the best—a deal I would take myself, and a willingness to put everything I said in writing. That's a compelling deal. That's on-the-spot innovation.

Around the office, we called it the "Airport Close."

Chapter 10

KEEP GOING, THINKING, PERSEVERING

Stick-to-itiveness isn't just a funny-sounding word; it's an essential attitude.

In Quality Systems' early days, Graeme and I worked 90 long, hard hours a week. We went through ups and downs, of course, as all companies do. Sometimes, in fact, the whole enterprise seemed to teeter on the edge, but we kept pushing forward, kept working, kept coming up with new ideas.

That's how entrepreneurs get through it. They get knocked down, they run into a stumbling block, they run out of money, whatever—but they pick themselves up and go forward. They "stick to it." They "hang in there."

They persevere.

My company is a prime example of repeated perseverance. Some of our first products were misdirected: the $16/month bowling system, the time-share dental service. We looked at the issues, gave them some concentrated attention, and figured out what we were doing wrong and how to turn things around to be successful. If we had just given up on those initial products, we'd still be selling our brains to make ends meet.

Our joint philosophies of being the best and never giving up helped us build one of our most successful enterprises. Quality Systems had developed a medical practice management system (PMS) with some limited electronic medical records (EMR) functionality on the minicomputer. By the early 1990s it dawned on us that personal computers (PCs) were not only the next wave in technology, they were becoming ubiquitous. We had to develop both a medical PMS and an EMR system that ran on the PC.

We tried to create a PC version of our system but could never get there. We were too steeped in the minicomputer culture. Our minicomputer system was the best, but its wave was coming to an end.

Don't Let What You Can't Do Stand in the Way of What You Do

I told Donn Neufeld, who ran our medical development group, "Look, for whatever reason, we can't build it. But we can't let that stop us. We need a PC-based system or we won't keep being the best. Why don't you go to a conference and find a company that already has a PC-oriented system that can interface with our minicomputer-based PMS? We'll buy the company and build on that."

So Donn canvassed several conferences and came upon Clinitec, run by Pat Cline. They had a working model of an EMR for the PC, but they were only doing about $500,000 in sales with no real growth forecast.

QSI cut a deal to buy 51 percent of Pat's company, which gave us control. (Later, on the advice of the investment company that did a secondary offering for us—a second issuance of our stock—we bought all of it.)

When he first came on board, Pat told me, "Shelly, you also need a companion practice-management product that runs on the PC."

We didn't have one. Neither did Pat. So we bought Micromed, Steve Puckett's company out of Atlanta, and merged the two enterprises into what later became our NextGen division.

At that point, the timing was right for a secondary offering. Markets open every once in a while that allow you to get a good price for your stock and get funds from the public to finance your future growth. When the market says, "There's an opening," you want to take it. That's when the investment company told me, "Shelly, you ought to buy the other 49 percent of Clinitec."

I said, "But I already control it."

And they wisely said, "It'll be much cheaper for you to buy it now, and it will also be a purpose for 'Use of Funds' for the secondary offering."

We had the right vision, the right product, and the right companies, but the promise of the EMR on which we'd based the secondary offering did not materialize as we'd envisioned. Our initial results did not fulfill our projections or our investors' expectations.

Our stock took a hit.

We could have broken up the division and sold it off in pieces. We could have abandoned the project altogether. But we didn't: we didn't give up, we didn't quit, we didn't throw in the towel. We knew we had the right product; we were just a little early. So, we persevered. We analyzed the situation from every angle and figured out what we were doing wrong. In time, this organization turned out to be enormously successful and a huge growth for us.

Had Pat sold his company to anybody but us, I believe it would have gone bankrupt. We gave his enterprise more than money; we gave them expertise on implementing and supporting turnkey systems. In fact, Quality Systems implemented his first system, for Tallahassee Ear Nose and Throat, or TNT, as we called it, which became an invaluable reference for him for the next five years.

Our logical next step was to get into the revenue-cycle management (RCM) business. We bought two companies right away, one out of St. Louis, the other out of Baltimore, merged them, and absorbed the enterprise into what is now our RCM division.

We initially had so many issues with the RCM business that Pat Cline got frustrated and wanted to throw in the towel. "Shelly, maybe we ought to sell these companies," he said. "This isn't working."

I said, "Absolutely not. This is a great, huge opportunity. Instead of ducking our head in the sand at the first sign of trouble, let's figure out what we're doing wrong and fix it so we can grow the companies."

Today that enterprise is another of Quality Systems' significant growth components.

"Always the best; always keep going" are essential attitudes for entrepreneurs. I remember an early conversation I had with Pat, who not only had an excellent technical background but was also an outstanding marketing and sales person. He said, "Well, Shelly, do you want me to grow the company or do you want me to make money?"

I answered, "It might be a novel idea to you, but we'd like you to do both—simultaneously."

And so he did.

Chapter 11

GOOD LUCK HELPS;
NO BAD LUCK HELPS MORE

Clever planning can never beat dumb luck.

In its early days, Federal Express, one of the great innovations of the last century, was losing over $1 million every month. When they reached the point that they couldn't pay their fuel bills, FedEx owner Fred Smith took the company's last $5,000 to Vegas and sat down at a blackjack table. By the end of the weekend, the company was up $32,000—enough to keep the planes in the air for a few more days, which was all the time Smith needed to raise additional funds.

When someone asked him what he'd been thinking taking such a chance with the company's money, Smith said, "What difference does it make? Without the funds for the plane fuel, we couldn't have flown anyway."

It doesn't matter how good a blackjack player Smith was; any game of chance is just that—chance. If he hadn't had some good luck that weekend at the tables, Federal Express would have been out of business almost before it got off the ground.

On the other hand, sometimes things are beyond your control.

You wind up on an airplane that crashes.

An unexpected government regulation that comes out of nowhere costs too much to keep your doors open.

Your building is taken out by a tsunami, an earthquake, or a tornado.

A trusted officer or director commits embezzlement or fraud.

Your industry's bubble bursts.

You didn't do anything wrong, but you're out of business. You can't control these things, you can't predict them or even prepare for them, but they're all possibilities. Would it help to have a contingency plan just in case a tornado flattens your building?

Probably—but it would probably also still close your doors.

Chapter 12

10X CHANGES

Whenever an industry experiences a 10X change in any component, the incumbents are in real trouble, and the new players on the block have a wide-open green field to make a fortune.

Andy Grove, the man who made Intel into the success it is, introduced the concept of technological 10X forces in his short book, *Only the Paranoid Survive* (Crown Business, 1999). This concept, which refers to the magnitude of the change, has nothing to do with luck, but it correlates with the idea that sometimes, things happen we simply cannot control.

When I started in business, I rode the minicomputer revolution. They did jobs that previously could only be handled by mid- and main-frame computers, so it was a green field for anyone who developed a new minicomputer application.

You can look into any industry—manufacturing, dentistry (where we went), medicine, stock brokers—and find the same thing. Whenever a revolutionary phase begins, anyone steeped in the new technology has a green field of opportunity.

Later, when the minicomputer was displaced by the personal computer (PC), the minicomputer leaders couldn't adapt. Major companies, such as Digital Equipment Corporation led by Ken Olsen, Edson de Castro's Data General Nova, and Wang Computers founded by Dr. An Wang and Dr. G.Y. Chu, all disappeared. They could not adapt their companies to the 10X change in technology.

Picture-Perfect Example

Since 1888, Eastman Kodak was the top name in film and film processing. A Fortune 500 company with an enormous market cap, Kodak was a household name all over the world, the veritable standard of photographic excellence. But in 2012, after 134 years in business and several in financial distress, the company went bankrupt. Why?

They were an incumbent in a radically altered field.

Historically, 86 percent of Kodak's business came from processing film. Even though an engineer at Kodak invented the first electronic camera in 1975, the company did not embrace that digital photography technology. Digital cameras hit the market in the 1990s but Kodak continued to focus on its historical revenue stream: film. By the mid-2000s, film had been almost wiped out by digital cameras, and when Apple released its first iPhone with built-in camera, the photo industry experienced a complete 10X change.

We don't develop film anymore. I don't carry around an album of pictures or snapshots in my wallet. My photos are right here on my iPhone and my iPad.

What did that mean to Kodak's film business? It ceased to exist, period. The entire industry was gone, wiped out in less than a decade. That's a 10X change. There was nothing Kodak could do to stay on top of the change; it could not scurry fast enough to replace the 86 percent of its business that no longer existed.

Keep in mind that the executives who ran Kodak and the other film/film processing companies were not stupid people. They were smart, they were talented; they were good businessmen and women. They had the basics of the technology, but they simply could not make the necessary transition. For one thing, they were too busy taking care of the day-to-day affairs of their existing business. They were totally immersed in the business and technology of film and film processing. Even if they had seen such an enormous change coming, they did not have the onboard talent, the culture, or the infrastructure to ride the new technological wave.

On the other hand, they also forgot the number one axiom of a successful business: **it has to be good for the customer**. For whatever reason, Kodak explicitly chose to not embrace the new technology. They drew their invisible line in the sand, in essence putting profit above what was best for the customer. Meanwhile, their competition moved forward. Apple first, and then the other various smart-technology companies did not have to alter anything to exploit the new picture-taking technology. They, too, were busy taking care of the affairs of their businesses, using their onboard talent, culture, and infrastructure to establish the new order of the day.

When a 10X industry change occurs, it can be very difficult for an established company to adapt, much less maintain its position in the marketplace. QSI had to transform itself three times: once from proprietary minicomputers to UNIX-based minicomputers; a second time from UNIX to networked-PC systems; and a third time from PCs to Internet software, a.k.a. the Cloud. Every one of these transformations has been huge and necessary.

We navigated the first transformation internally and the second by buying a company that had the technology. The third transformation involved buying intellectual property from a company and expanding on it using our internal expertise and skills.

Chapter 13

DON'T PUSH, INSPIRE

*"Shelly, you got me to do things I never knew
I was capable of doing!"*

Handling people is a huge, huge element of any business, the most difficult thing in the world. The failed-business junkyard is littered with companies whose owners or CEOs thought they could run an organization even though they had no people skills. All the technical knowledge and financial acumen in the world will not help you keep key employees or inspire those who do stay with you to succeed. When your employees do things they never thought they could do—when they exceed their own expectations—it creates yet another win-win.

Successful companies are grown in win-win environments.

Part of your leadership is to inspire people to do things that are extraordinary for them, to do things they didn't know they could do but would never break them, to encourage them to stretch past their comfort zone and perform "above their heads."

> I know you may have never done this before—it's all new to you—but you should be able to do it. I'm not telling you to run the mile in two minutes. I believe that's impossible, and I'd never ask you to do what I believe is impossible. But hey, you're a superfast runner! You could do a five-minute mile, right? Here are some hints on how to get there. Now go figure it out, do all the work involved, practice, and you'll get there.

Inspiration is all about your belief in an individual's ability to do just that: to push themselves beyond their own self-image, past their self-imposed limitations, and through their fears and self-deprecation.

On the other hand, I never assign someone a job I don't think they can do. You have to know how to inspire without driving someone too much, and you have to know the difference. It's a fine line and a common judgment call. Any "push" or "drive" should come from the person's own desire to accomplish, to live up to your expectations and trust.

That's inspiration. That's leadership.

Motivation

Motivating people is easy when times are good. The company's success reflects in each individual's success.

But what about when times are tough, when you're in deep trouble and feel like you have to solve all the problems of the world? How do you motivate your staff to become part of the team that gets you out of trouble?

You tell them the truth: that you've been through trouble before and have come out of it. Assure them there's light ahead, a pot of gold waiting at the end of the rainbow, and that you're going to find it, even though you're experiencing a "dark hour" right now.

Share your vision. Make sure your people know what you're working toward—all of you, collectively. It will take the whole team to turn things around. Give them unbelievable encouragement: everyone's contribution is important.

Never avoid your staff or employees during tough times. Foster the same sense of "we're all in this together" culture that everyone enjoys during good times. This is when your open-door, first-name policies will really pay off. Now is the time to stay very close to your people, to seek out and offer individual encouragement. When a person feels "part of," they instinctively push for the team's success.

Chapter 14

LEARNING COMES FROM ANALYSIS

*Spend 10 percent of the time thinking about your problems
and 90 percent of the time thinking about solving them.*

A lot of people say, well I got this problem, I got that problem.
They spend 90 percent of the time thinking about the problems they
have and 10 percent on solving them. It should be reversed. They
should be spending 90 percent on figuring out what they are going
to do.

I like to learn as many things as I can from every mistake,
circumstance, and incident I experience. That turns the "lose" of
the situation around to at least a partial "win." You want to learn
all the lessons you possibly can from anything that didn't come out
completely right, not just one or two.

Think of it this way: you had a bad result from a project or with a potential client or business arrangement. You got through it, but it cost you something. You've already paid the tuition; you might as well learn the lessons! And if you multiply your lessons exponentially—10 x 10 x 10—your growth will be leaps and bounds beyond the person who learns one lesson per experience and then stops. He's growing linearly; you're growing exponentially.

All our clients have maintenance plans with us, which involves a monthly fee. We noticed some people would not pay their maintenance fee, but wanted to get back on the plan when they had maintenance requirements.

That's like dropping your insurance and then wanting to reinstate it retroactively to cover the damage when lightning hits your roof.

That didn't seem fair to us, so we analyzed why it was happening. What could we do to change the situation so it was to the customer's advantage to pay their maintenance?

We analyzed our contracts. The language allowed customers to drop their maintenance and return at will, and we would take care of anything that had happened in the interim.

No wonder we were losing money on these clients.

We instituted a new policy. If the customer went off maintenance and wanted to come back on, they had to pay all the maintenance they would have paid during the lapse plus a reconnection fee or premium. That made it non-advantageous to do what was unfair. By doing the analysis and implementing a strategy based on that analysis, we solved the problem.

We had another problem in our early years. Our system contracts included a payment schedule, such as 10 percent of the contract value up front, then 20 percent at such-and-such a point, and so on until the contract was paid in full.

We noticed people weren't paying us according to the terms they'd signed. We had a standard 5 percent interest clause, but it was such a nominal amount that it didn't prevent anyone from missing payments.

I always told my customers that we'd do anything for them. We'd work 24 hours a day for them, if necessary. The only thing they had to do was pay us according to the terms they agreed to.

Once again, it wasn't fair, and we were losing money on these clients.

So we analyzed the problem and realized that it was actually advantageous for the customer to just "drag" us: they got a cheap loan on the system *and* they got the system.

As a result of that analysis, we changed our contract terms. Normally, we gave our customers a 10 percent discount on our systems; if the customer bought a $200,000 system, we gave him $20,000 off. Now we added language that said,

> If you're late on any payment, we'll inform you. If you don't remit in 30 days, you not only owe the payment with interest, you also owe the discount we gave you, because that was part of a package that included your paying on time.

So if they were late, we'd give them notice of a 30-day grace period to get caught up. Otherwise, we could demand the full, undiscounted price.

When we first put this into our contracts, some of our salesmen said, "Shelly, we won't be able to sell systems if we do this!"

I said, "Wait a minute—what guy is going to look you in the eye and say, 'I'm not going to pay you according to the terms' at the beginning of the contract? If he does, give him the names of our competitors and tell him to take their business to them."

First Hypothesize, Then Do a *Gedankenexperiment (Thought Experiment)*

Whenever you analyze anything, be it a business, political, or personal situation, replay your proposed change to see if a) it will cure the situation and b) it will have any unintended consequences of its own.

If the people in Washington did that, businesses wouldn't have so many regulations to contend with that don't actually solve anything. A prime example occurred when the Enron scandal hit and Congress imposed the Draconian Sarbanes-Oxley (SOX), which is a huge burden on a lot of companies. And yet, not only did it not solve the intended problem, it created more problems.

SOX was passed to protect investors from corporations' fraudulent accounting practices. Its 66 pages comprise a series of rules and regulations about what records to keep, how to keep them, and how long they have to be stored, all in an attempt to stop companies from lying about their real financial status.

If Congress had done a *gedankenexperiment*—a thought experiment to consider the possible consequences, good or bad, they might have realized that record-keeping won't stop people from lying, and, in fact, just provides another vehicle for obstructing the truth.

A simpler and more effective solution would have been to make the top officials, the CEOs and president, personally responsible: "Put your revenue, your profit, and your adjusted cash flow for the past three years on one piece of paper. If you lie on that paper, that constitutes fraud, and you'll serve a mandatory sentence of a year in prison."

That would solve the problem, because CEOs and presidents don't want to go to jail. That's the value of a *gedankenexperiment.*

Chapter 15

"I WAS WRONG"

*If you cannot admit you made a mistake, you cannot grow.
It's that simple.*

Analyzing any situation, be it top-level corporate fraud, middle-management miscalculation, or contract inequities, requires the ability to say, "I was wrong."

I learned this with my management team: the only people who could grow were the ones who could admit their mistakes. If an individual couldn't own up to their error about something that had happened, they absolutely could not grow. They were ceilinged, stuck wherever they were in their career, in the company, and probably in their personal life as well.

You can easily recognize this type of person. They're the ones who always look for someone to blame whenever something goes wrong or doesn't turn out as expected: it was Joe's fault, it was Jimmy's fault. The customer didn't understand the system. The tech made a mistake. Somebody else didn't get it right.

They can't contribute to a situational analysis because their ability to look at all the angles of a problem stops at assigning blame for whatever went wrong. Whenever I encounter someone whose insecurities won't let them admit they made an error, I know I cannot challenge them to become more than they are at the moment.

All that changes the minute the person can walk into the room, talk to their peers, and say, "You know what? I made a mistake. It wasn't three-quarters my mistake; it was *entirely* my mistake. I was wrong. And with what I've learned from it, I won't do it again."

I've found over my career that when someone who usually places the blame on others or on circumstances makes the leap to say, "I was wrong. I wasn't half wrong, I wasn't maybe wrong, I was wrong," it's huge. Doors open, vision clears, and they begin to rise like a helium-filled balloon. They can soar to the heights, all because of that one item, that one ability to look at their peers and say, "You know what? I was wrong."

It might sound like a simple thing, but I have observed and witnessed it over and over in my company. The minute they passed that height, that self-imposed limitation, all of sudden their growth was exponential, they shot up to the sky. The people who can't do that just cannot grow.

If they can't grow, they can't be successful, and if they can't be successful, they can't add to the company's success.

I was wrong about the dentist's time-share being the right answer.

I was wrong that selling to the bowling leagues was the way to go.

I was wrong that our in-house people could create the PC-based EMR system we needed.

It's the ability to look reality in the face and not have an ego problem about saying, "I had this idea, and it had these fatal flaws. That's the reason it didn't work. I was wrong. But I'm going to correct it and get it right"—that's possibly the most essential ability an entrepreneur, leader, director, manager, or employee can have.

Chapter 16

NEVER OFFER A DEAL YOU WOULDN'T TAKE YOURSELF

Good ethics is good business. If you make a good ethical decision, it is a good business decision.

Even if you don't know anything about business, you can be sure that if you make a good ethical decision, it will be a good business decision. Good ethics and good business are interchangeable. If you want to be a good business person, you have to make ethical decisions. It's the only way you will succeed.

When I enter into a business situation with another individual, it has to be a win-win for both of us. It can never be I win-you lose. Often, it takes some creativity to figure out how to make sure the deal is good for the customer and good for me.

I've found the best way to ensure that is to figure out the deal I'd want if I were the customer. Whether you look at it from the ethics angle or from the business angle, you'll always end up with a win-win situation if you never offer your clients a deal you wouldn't take yourself.

If you wouldn't buy what you're offering, it's not a good deal. In the end, it's always about the customer: what will this product, this service, this deal I'm putting together do for my customer? If it isn't the best deal for the best product or the best service, I wouldn't take it—so why should my customer?

Chapter 17

MAKE IT EASY TO BUY
AND EASY TO USE

This is a true story. It really happened just this way.

I thought this concept was so intuitive it did not need to be mentioned, until I had a frustrating experience in Laguna Beach, where I now live.

I own a Tesla, a completely electric car. It's not a hybrid; if you don't have electricity, the car doesn't run. I had a special outlet installed at my home to charge the vehicle, but for whatever reason, it didn't work one day when I needed to charge my car.

My wife Janet said, "Shelly, there's a place downtown with two charging stations just for the city of Laguna Beach. It's right across from Anastasia."

Anastasia was a favorite restaurant of ours, so we decided to have some breakfast while the car was charging.

The sign at the station said, "$2 an Hour." I'm reasonably literate when it comes to technology, so I looked around for a place to insert or swipe my credit card and start charging my car. Parking meters all over the city have that functionality. You swipe, the fee gets added to your credit card, and off you go.

That's called easy.

But I couldn't find the meter's credit card slot. I wanted to use it—I wanted to give my money to this company and purchase their product—but I couldn't figure out how.

Luckily, they had a telephone number for support. I dialed and a woman answered. I told her my problem and she asked, "What station are you at?"

"I don't know. I'm in Laguna. How many stations do you have in Laguna?"

She didn't know, so she started asking a series of questions for which I had no answers. We finally worked through her entire list of queries, at which point she said, "You're in Laguna Beach."

I knew that. I'd said that at the beginning of our conversation. I'd now spent almost five minutes being unable to buy this company's product.

I said, "Okay, now we both know where I am. I'd like to use this meter to charge my car. How can I use my credit card?"

"Oh, you need one with a special chip."

"I don't have a credit card with a special chip."

"Well, you need to go buy one."

I took a deep breath and said, "Look, I just want to charge my car. What can I do?"

"Well, since you don't have a credit card with a special chip, we have to do a different process."

"Can I give the credit card information to you?"

"No, I'm not allowed to do that. I have to send you to another company to take that information."

Again, I swear: this is a true story.

She transferred me to her credit-card company, where a recording told me to press this number to get here and that number to get there. It took three times for it to accept my credit card. Finally, the system accepted my card and transferred me back to the original lady.

I said, "Okay, my card is on file; now how do I get the device off the meter so I can charge my car?"

She said, "Well, you took so long, you have to reinitialize it."

*I t*ook so long!?

She walked me through pushing another series of buttons until the device finally came off the meter. I plugged it into my car—and…

Nothing. Because I'm reasonably literate when it comes to technical issues, I knew I was supposed to see a flashing green light. I told the woman the car wasn't charging.

She said, "Oh yeah, I have to reinitialize it on my end now."

The whole process took somewhere between ten and fifteen minutes versus the couple of seconds I should have spent inserting my card in the meter.

This was the epitome of *not* making it easy to buy.

A Different Experience

When I was starting out in my company, I made cold calls to sell my brains as a technical manager.

Cold calling was the hardest job in the world for me at that time. I picked up the local newspaper every day and looked through the want ads to see who needed software help. When I reached John Vogelpol at Bourns, he already knew how good I was, and if he could, he said, he'd hire me on the spot. I said I wasn't looking to be an employee; I was offering my services as a software consultant.

He said, "I'd love to have you do this, Shelly, but I'd have to write a purchase order and get it signed by the management."

I said, "John, let me make it easy for you. I'll write the purchase order myself. All you'll have to do is get it signed."

And that's what I did. I saw his need, I knew I could fulfill it, so I did it all for him. His transaction to buy was the time it took for him and his boss to write their names. That was it.

If I'd been an electric-car-charging meter, I would have had their credit card information in less time than it took to write this sentence.

Make it Easy

Before I could get my own business started, a friend of mine, Jerry Burnett, who also co-founded Avistar Communications and Vicor Inc., asked me to join his company, Index Systems. The company was headquartered in Cambridge, Massachusetts, but Jerry said, "I know you like California. We're opening up a California office, so come back here and live for a while, get to know the company, and maybe this will be what you're looking for and you won't have to start your own business. You can just move to our California office."

Index Systems was run by Thomas Gerrity, who had a PhD from the MIT Sloan School of Management and later served as the Dean of the Wharton School of Business at the University of Pennsylvania. Jerry had a PhD from Princeton. The rest of the Index Systems principals were all MIT whiz kids as well.

When I arrived, Index System had a thriving consulting business selling Portfolio Management Systems to clients like Bank of America and making money hand over fist. Highly successful. I didn't know what I could contribute. Tom said, "Shelly, would you look at this Documate product we have?"

Documate was a word processor created by Dan Diamond. I took a look at it and said, "Tom, this product is going nowhere."

"What do you mean? It's a great new technology. It was designed by a PhD."

I said, "And that's the problem: you need a PhD to run it. It's not easy to use. It was built for a highly technical person, but the market for word processing is the guy on the street with a high school education."

Tom was devastated. They'd been pouring all their profits from highly successful components into Documate, and it was draining the company. The fundamental design made it too difficult to use, making it almost impossible to sell.

Index Systems dumped the product and went on to grow a thriving business.

There's a postscript to this story. After a year with Index, I decided my real dream in life was to own and run my own company. So I walked into Tom Gerrity's office and said, "I'm going back to California."

"What do you have going in California?"

"Nothing. I just have a dream."

He said, "Do you realize how many businesses fail the first year? You're bucking the odds! How can you do something like that? You have a wife and kids."

I said, "Tom, I have a dream. And I've discovered who I am. I've got to have my own company. That's it. As far as being set up with a whole bunch of things in California, I don't have a thing. I just have a dream."

He found it difficult to understand how I could go for a dream, but forty years later, I can categorically say I made the right choice.

So I moved my family back to Corona, California, into the same house I'd leased out a year earlier, and started my own company out of the back room. After I'd hired a few people, I came to find we needed word-processing capabilities.

By that time, I had hired four or five top-notch people from my days at Rockwell, including a tech guru named Don Pearson. I told him, "I need you to design a word processor, but let me give you the criteria: I want whoever walks through that door—anybody, someone who doesn't know me, who's never seen a computer in their life—and in sixty seconds I want them to be able to write a letter and print it."

So, that's what we built: a word processor so easy to use anyone could learn it in under a minute. We used it as part of our evaluation process when we interviewed secretaries; it was one of the work horses of our company. And this word processor, designed in the 1970s, is still in use with some of our clients to this day. It was that good.

We built it on the principle called WYSIWYG: What You See Is What You Get. On our word processor, what appeared on the screen is what you got. It didn't have other components or abilities embedded in it. It was an easy-learn/easy-use word processor that anyone with sixty seconds of instruction could utilize.

Eventually, we made the system so sophisticated that people could run their billing on it. It had a lot of the functions that were later introduced by Lotus 123 and the early versions of Excel. We had all those features back in the '70s with the WYSIWYG.

Easy to buy, easy to use.

Chapter 18

ONE HOUR A WEEK

As CEO, dedicate meeting once a week with your top people.

One hour. Anybody can find one hour in one day if they can count on it being a one-hour meeting. In QSI's early days, our meetings would ramble for hours. I finally said, "In return for your commitment to attend, we will limit the meeting to one hour. What we don't accomplish we'll push over to next week."

Some people said, "But I'll be out of town that day. I can't make the meeting."

And I replied, "There's a telephone everywhere in America. Call in."

Today, of course, there is no spot on earth so remote that someone cannot communicate by telephone, cell phone, iPad, or computer interface. Everyone must attend.

I used to hold my staff meetings every Friday. Everyone had to talk about their problems, achievements, plans, and so forth. No one was allowed to claim they had nothing to say.

I used those meetings to tell my senior staff what I, as CEO, knew that they might not collectively know, to transfer information from me to them. Then they transferred information they knew to me and everyone else. Everyone had to report something about their operation.

We never came out of that meeting without someone learning something important they hadn't known walking in.

Often, I came in with a problem I wanted my senior staff to solve. I also gave them an answer I'd thought of, which I knew wasn't the best solution but which let everyone know that this was a solvable problem.

"Our company has this predicament. This is a possible solution. Can anyone talk about better ideas?"

That's when the fireworks happened.

We started by writing everybody's ideas up on the board—with no critiquing allowed. I wanted to empower their ingenuity, not disturb their creative juices.

After we collected everyone's ideas—however many there were, however long it took—we went back and looked at each one logically, analyzing them with a *gedankenexperiment* approach: will this idea actually solve the problem without causing more problems?

In every instance, the group's collective answer was much better than the one I had, which I was very humbly honored to acknowledge. I basically tapped into the genius of these twelve top, bright executives to help me get to a point I couldn't have gotten to myself. I felt like an orchestra leader, conducting my people to play at their virtuoso best.

Even after I was no longer the CEO, as Chairman of the Board I encouraged my successor to continue this practice. I believe he also found these regular Friday meetings extremely valuable.

Public Floggings

We often had meetings that included all segments of the company: sales, support—everyone. One day Grant Sadler, our top salesman, turned to Donn Neufeld, the head of our support division, and said, "Donn, you did a terrible thing with this client. They called me and said you screwed up their system."

Donn immediately protested, which started a heated discussion, and I thought, "This is just wrong."

I told Grant, "Look, you don't know that Donn screwed up anything, yet here you have accused him in front of all these people. The only thing you know for a fact is that so-and-so from XYZ group made these statements to you. They may be true, they may be half true, they may be completely false, but the truth is, you don't know."

I said, "I'll tell you what, Grant. We'll investigate the situation and report to you next week. But don't ever lynch somebody again without hearing all sides of the story first."

In that case, we discovered that one of the customer's employees had actually been the one who messed up everything and tried to blame it on our company. The mess-up we could handle. The bigger issue was Grant making the leap from hearing the allegation to accepting it as true to making a public accusation.

These kinds of issues come up now and then in every company. Sometimes there's a sliver of truth to the claim; sometimes it's half true. Over the years, we found all shades of everything. The key point is to uncover the full truth before you make any accusation at all, much less a public one.

The Delphi Method

That big lesson came out of our staff meetings. So did what I call "the Delphi Method."

It started out as an experiment. We had to make a decision about promoting someone, so I asked this group of twelve people, "How good is this person? Is this a good person, or someone not worthy of promotion? Give me a measure of his goodness on a scale of one to ten. What do you really think?"

Everyone asked, "What criteria should we use?"

I said, "No specific criteria. Just give me your overall impression of the person."

So that none of us would know or be influenced by what anyone else said, everyone wrote their answer on a slip of paper, folded it up, and threw it into a box. I opened them all at the same time. I figured at least I'd know what everyone thought about that individual.

The results were amazing. I'm a mathematician, so I know that the odds of twelve people's random numbers all clustering around the same answer (plus or minus one) is close to zero. But every time we used this tactic, that's what happened.

I called it the Delphi Method after the Greek oracle at Delphi who spoke for Apollo and whose answers helped the city grow wealthy and powerful.

It allowed us to make quick decisions, but I wondered why such a simple technique returned such correlation. After some consideration, I realized I was getting the combined contemplation, smoothing, and normalization of each individual's deliberations. They were processing a lot of information to produce their answer, and all their answers clustered around whatever number.

Occasionally, the answers clustered around eight or nine, for example, but one person wrote down "two." When we investigated, we always discovered that the odd man out didn't understand something about the candidate, something peculiar to that outlier. Still, the odds of achieving that kind of correlation on a number within a scale of one to ten is truly amazing, but we did.

Chapter 19

TRUST EVERYONE, BUT CUT THE CARDS

A precautionary tale. The names have been changed to protect the innocent and guilty.

Sandy came into my office and sat down. She looked uncomfortable. Finally, she said, "Look, I've been having an affair with Johnny. He told me he was getting a divorce and I got tired of waiting, so I called his wife and asked, 'When is the divorce coming?' She said, 'What divorce?' When he found out, he said, 'I'll get you fired.'"

I said, "Nobody's firing you. Don't worry about that. Get your life together."

As she was walking out the door, she turned around and said, "By the way, he's running a business out of your New Jersey office."

"What is it?"

She said, "I don't know, but he's doing something out there."

I had a board meeting that day, so I told Donn Neufeld to get on our New Jersey computer via a telecommunication modem link and take a look.

He said, "Look for what?"

I said, "I don't know. Just look around and tell me what you find."

Donn dialed into New Jersey, got online, and discovered that Johnny had been using my facility and my parts to invoice other companies and pocket the money. He was clever about it, too. If anybody dialed into his system, he knew about it. He disconnected us; we spent the afternoon getting on and being kicked off.

Finally I turned to Graeme. "Will you do me a favor? Get on a plane and go to New Jersey, tonight. Take a red-eye."

I always keep keys to all the facilities at our corporate office, so I told him, "Don't let anyone in. Lock down the room. Get on their computer, and find out what's going on. Here's the data I have for you so far."

Graeme flew to New Jersey and ingeniously took their back-up tape and compared its files to what was on the computer. Because they had a setup to watch exactly what was being done on their modem connections, they saw they were under suspicion and had tried to erase everything that night while Graeme was en route—but that backfired.

It actually led Graeme right to the incriminating evidence they thought they had erased!

We later referred the case to the New Jersey District Attorney, but their office said, "We're fighting the Mafia; this is too low-profile for us."

That same person, Johnny, had been a guest in my house. He and his wife had been guests on my boat. We fired him, but we didn't know how deep the conspiracy was at that point, which is why I sent Graeme and only Graeme. I trust him with my life. Everyone needs someone they can turn to without fear, whose trustworthiness, loyalty, and abilities are beyond reproach.

We fired a few other people at the same time who were involved, but to this day we don't know exactly how deep the conspiracy went. Johnny had been running a business out of our facilities, using our employees to sell our parts and service his clients, and pocketing the money for himself.

His dishonesty got caught in our open-communication web. Just a bit of poetic justice.

Beginnings November 1973 – October 1976. QSI's early consulting projects included systems with extensive telecommunications (computer modem at top), development of a bowling league sheet processing system and systems using marked card reading devices.

1979, at my desk, hard at work as the President of Quality Systems, Inc.

1973: QSI's first in-house
computer was the size
of a refrigerator.

1975: QSI's first
office location
on 17th Street in
Tustin, CA

In 1977 Quality Systems installed its first minicomputer system at the Riverside Dental Group in Riverside, CA. They are still a QSI client today.

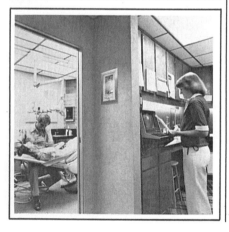

1983 standing next to turnkey minicomputer system.

1983 Graeme Frehner, my friend and technology genius.

Computers from 1986 that housed QSI systems. This was state of the art technology and was considered "compact and space-efficient" equipment.

Awarded the 2009 Excellence in Entrepreneurship (EIE) award from the Orange County Business Journal. Judges were asked to identify individuals with impressive and extraordinary vision, execution, accomplishments and potential for success.

NASDAQ Stock Market Opening Bell Ceremony in honor of QSI's 35th year in business.

Received the Ernst & Young 2009 Entrepreneur of the Year in Healthcare category for Orange County/Desert Cities Program and was a Finalist at the national level. This award honors entrepreneurs whose ingenuity, hard work and perseverance have created and sustained successful growing business ventures. One of 10 winners across seven categories.

In 2010 QSI won the Growth Award in the public company category from The Association for Corporate Growth Orange County Chapter (ACG OC). The Award recognizes companies that have exhibited distinctive strategic positioning as well as sustainable growth and profitability during the past two years.

Accepting the TechAmerica's 52nd Annual Innovator Award in 2010 in the Software category, which honors eight innovators from different industries for their contributions to the technology sector.

2011 in Abu Dhabi at the 8th Annual International Business Awards (IBA), the "Stevies". QSI received three awards in the categories of Company of the Year in the field of Computer Services, Best Video in the field of Technology Sales, and Information Technology Executive of the Year.

2009 Giving my acceptance speech after being presented the Gold Stevie at the American Business Awards for Chairman of the Year; Management Category; Nomination Title: Sheldon Razin: Visionary, Entrepreneur And Healthcare Information Technology Pioneer.

IBA also awarded QSI the People's Choice award as Favorite Computer Services Company and received a Distinguished Honoree nod for Chairman of the Year.

June 3, 2014
NASDAQ Closing
Bell Ceremony
in honor of QSI's
40th business
anniversary.

June 3, 2014 QSI Management team at NASDAQ Closing Bell Ceremony in honor of QSI's 40th business anniversary.

Chapter 20

KEEP CONTROL

A great idea is worth one point. Being able to execute it is worth 99 points.

One of the most dangerous elements of a company is figuring out how to bootstrap your way into and through business. That's a tough question, and there is no one, single answer. What QSI did was start out by selling what we had—our brains—until we had enough revenue to create products so we could sell those using whatever contacts we had. We always knew the Holy Grail was to have products that people needed to buy. Until you have products to sell, you don't have a business; you have a consulting enterprise, a freelance endeavor.

Investors

The decisions you make to keep your company on the right track and to avoid those paths that lead into debt or insolvency are key for any entrepreneur. One of the first and biggest siren songs you'll encounter, especially if you have a technology company, is venture capital. Entire organizations are built around teaching people how to pitch to lenders and investors, bringing entrepreneurs into contact with lenders and investors, and creating entrepreneur/investor networks. As appealing as that "free, easy" money may seem, I endorse the advantages of staying out of debt and obligation-free.

> *Bootstrap your business. Sell what you have, not what you want to have or plan to have two years from now. Keep fixed expenses and all salaries, including yours, low.*

This is a fundamental principle, one I've watched too many people ignore. They expend their energies wooing investors, and then waste the money when they get it. Their focus isn't on selling what they have or building their business. It's on enticing other people to give them money. But venture capitalists generally (and reasonably) want control over what happens with their money. They want to take that all-important 51 percent of the companies in which they invest. Eight out of ten businesses fail within the first year, and I believe loss of control plays a big part in those failures.

Why put yourself under that burden? If there's money left at the end of the year, you can always distribute the cash. Meanwhile, especially when you're just starting out, pay yourself and your key people a below-market salary and keep your expenses at a minimum. That's why so many successful businesses start in the owner's back room or garage—and why so many profligate businesses, no matter how great their core idea is, never get off the ground.

Lenders

When you borrow, the fate of your company is dependent on whomever loaned you the money, so if you possibly can, stay out of debt. After all, debt is just a timing difference. You have to pay the money back sometime, so you might as well save your own cash to spend when you need it.

Banks are in the business of making money for the bank, not for you, no matter what they claim in their advertisements. The next time you want to consider taking out a loan, ask to look at one of your bank's contracts. You'll find an assortment of Draconian clauses buried in the fine print on page thirteen or forty-eight that allows the lender to do things you never imagined, just because you've borrowed its money. They can come in and look at your balance sheet, for example, and say, "Oh, it's changed, so we're calling your loan."

Your loan officer may assure you the bank will never exercise that clause, but six months later when he's moved to another company, his assurances will be as useful as empty air.

I advise new entrepreneurs to sell their brains, call family and friends, do whatever they must to get funding without losing control of at least 51 percent of their company. Fifty-one percent: that's the magic ownership number. It may be tough, and you may not be able to do it, but you want to keep at least 51 percent of your company, no matter how you raise your funding.

Otherwise, you've lost control.

Chapter 21

PRODUCT IDEAS SOURCES

An entrepreneur has to be flexible enough to let his company morph into its best configuration.

I've informally researched different companies and have found they started in one area and ended up in another. It's almost universal. A company starts out with certain ideas about what it is and what it offers, but then morphs into something else.

Which is exactly what QSI did.

We started out with one set of products and then morphed in a totally different direction. Today, many of our product ideas evolve from our annual user meetings.

As with everything we do, our user meetings are good for everyone involved. The company sells products to new and existing customers. The employees get ideas about effects, improvements, and new products from having face-to-face meetings with customers and vendors. Our vendor business partners sell their products and services to our customers. And our customers interface with our experts, get product usage answers, offer new ideas, and network and forge relationships with other customers and QSI employees. They come away with a better understanding of our product lines, our services, and the future of our company.

That makes it a win-win-win-win situation—you can't ask for anything better than that!

Chapter 22

ACQUIRE TALENT

Keep it personal.

Acquiring talent as a small company is the most difficult thing you have to do. I have a principle for it: keep it personal.

When I started Quality Systems I was one man; I started it by myself. I looked through my Rolodex of friends, of the people I respected and admired. I went first for the people I'd worked with in the past. That's how I found Graeme. I had known him not only from being a close friend for years, but also from his background at Rockwell. I knew how brilliant he was, what a genius he was, and I knew he was compatible with my culture. We both wanted to be the best. Not good; the best. I knew I was good at developing software, but somebody with that kind of genius would be invaluable in getting this company off the ground. I picked up the phone and called him. I told him my vision, but I knew he had a bunch of kids so I was completely honest with him. "Graeme, you know it's a risky venture."

He said, "Shelly, I have confidence in you."

Graeme became my partner almost immediately.

The second thing I did was reach out to anybody and everybody for personal referrals. I'd approach people at every party and social environment I attended. "Hey I'm looking for people like this. Do you know anybody?"

I can still go through our organization and tell you where most of our people came from. As a matter of fact, one of the people still with us, Donn Neufeld, has been with us since just a few years after we incorporated. I was led to him by the son of a friend.

The friend was John Weissman, whom I knew from my Rockwell days. I saw him at a party and told him I was looking for people. He said, "You ought to hire my son, Bruce."

Bruce was very sharp, so I hired him. One day Bruce told me, "I want you to hire this person I know. His name is Donn Neufeld."

I said, "I don't even have a position."

He said, "I don't care. This guy is so good you have to hire him."

Donn started in client support, he had a technical background as well, and he too had a personal culture of excellence. He's now head of our Dental and EDI (Electronic Data Interchange) divisions.

The toughest way to get good talent is from recruiters. All our good talent, our most valuable people, came from this referral game, from spreading the word around to personal contacts. If you think you might one day start a new business, keep a good Rolodex and stay up to date on their phone numbers. When the opportunity arises, call. Even if they can't do the job, they might be able to refer someone.

What does it cost you to tell people what you need? Nothing.

I met Grant Sadler, who eventually became QSI's head of sales, because our first salesman was on a ski lift with Grant's wife Jeanne and they got to talking about computer use in dentistry. He said he wasn't having any luck selling our timeshare product to dentists, and Jeanne said, "My husband runs the Riverside Dental Group and is a past president of the Dental Group Management Association (DGMA). Maybe you should talk to him."

Grant lived and breathed selling; he just loved the game. No one loved his work more than Grant. And his personal culture matched ours: we sell nothing but the best.

When I first wanted Grant to work for me, the Riverside Dental Group said, "Gee, if we contribute one of our officers, we'd like to have exclusive marketing rights."

I told them, "I'll give you exclusive marketing rights provided you sell a minimum of this amount. Otherwise, you lose the exclusive."

"No problem; we can sell thousands."

"Well, if you sell a fraction of that, you keep your exclusive."

They meant well, but their demand essentially gave me the ability to deal fairly with what I suspected would happen: "If you don't sell, I want to be able to sell."

They agreed, and we hired Grant with their permission; in fact, he headed up our sales and marketing. He provided a need and a capability wrapped in a culture that matched our own, and, of course, he was extremely talented and very hard-working—just like all the really successful people in my company.

We did a lot of business the first year with Grant. I asked him, "What do we need to do to double our business?"

He said, "I need to hire some more talent."

So then he introduced me to Don Clay and Patti Lavoie, whom we hired the second year. Don was also a former president of DGMA, and Patti was a specialist in Sales Assistance and Implementation.

The next year I said, "What else do we need to do?" and Grant introduced me to Bill Casanova, another former DGMA president. So our entire sales force was well-connected in the dentistry world.

I hired the best so I could deliver the best.

Chapter 23

REPLACE YOURSELF

High Risk Replacement: hire today, start tomorrow, fingers crossed. Low Risk Replacement: train someone else to do be you, one job at a time.

A company cannot grow unless you develop a succession plan at all levels.

Entrepreneurs come to me and say, "Shelly, I don't know what to do. I'm working 90 hours a week, and I'm the only guy that can do X, Y, Z in this company. It's killing me! I can't grow beyond myself and three or four people."

I know exactly what they're talking about. When I started my company, I did everything. But I eventually realized that only way to grow the company was to get someone else to do the things I was doing.

That was very hard for me, because I had a high bar of excellence they'd have to achieve. It was much easier for me to just do everything than to get someone else to do it the way I wanted it done.

One classic example was our contracts. I knew I could learn the necessary legal language quicker and easier than a lawyer could learn my business, so I had an attorney write our very first contract, then I said, "Tell you what, I'll write the next one. You critique it, only change what's necessary, and tell me why you changed it."

From then on I wrote and signed all the contracts.

But I couldn't grow reviewing and signing all the company's contracts—we had too many. So I called in Greg Flynn and said, "Greg I'd like you to do this now."

He said, "I can't do what you've been doing. I don't know how to do it."

I said, "I want you to do it, so here's how we'll handle it. I'll prep you in advance so you'll have some knowledge under your belt. Then you'll be a fly on the wall while I negotiate the contract. Afterwards, we'll review it together. The next time, I'll be a fly on the wall while you do it. We might have to do it multiple times, but when I'm confident you can do it as good as or better than me, I'm never going to do it again. I'll be out of that business. When we finish this, you'll have the authority to sign contracts. I've never given that to anybody else. You'll have it."

And that's what we did. I explained the principles of our contracts: no open-ended or ambiguous statements; tight, specific language; no clauses of "killer" liability. I talked to him about how I negotiate contracts: start by writing all the money issues on one side of the paper and the non-money issues on the other, then prioritize. Then he shadowed me once or twice, I shadowed him for a while, and that was it.

I wasn't taking any risks because I could observe that Greg was able to do the job as well as or better than I could. If he hadn't been able to do it, I wouldn't have turned over the responsibility to him. I'd have told him, "Greg, you're not cut out for this. You're a very valuable employee, you give great value to the company, but this isn't one of your strong suits." Then I'd have found someone else.

But I'd never have started with Greg if I didn't think he was capable of doing the job. Yes, it was a stretch for him; yes, he was frightened and didn't think he could handle it. But I believed he could do it, and together we proved the succession process worked.

Chapter 24

OPEN DEPARTMENTS

There we were in 1977, a technical company with a unique product that was revolutionizing dentistry. As we were putting it in at Riverside Dental Group, I realized, "If I don't train these people and support them forever, they will fail."

So I created the Client Managing, Training, and Support departments. Then I created the Field Service and Conversion departments.

The field service business wasn't core to us. We'd been using third parties to maintain and fix our customer's computers for them, but we decided to bring it in-house for a number of reasons. First, we wanted control of the quality. Second, it was a great money-maker in terms of revenue/profit/cash flow. So when we looked at the growth of the company and the concept of field service, we realized that one person couldn't do it all. He just couldn't. We needed a department to handle the volume.

So I hired somebody who had been doing a good job at field service for one of my service vendors, and from that was born our Field Service department. The key is to find a head who can then hire the people under him to do the job with the quality you expect.

When we delivered our first systems, our client management, training, and implementation was handled as one thing. Later, we broke them into three departments: Client Management, Training & Implementation, and Data Conversion. Business was too brisk to create departments first and then hope for revenue to support them after the fact. We created the departments as the need arose.

Departments Arise Organically

At the end of our first year, I told Grant, our salesman, "Next year, we need to double or triple what we just did."

He said, "I'll have to hire some people."

I said, "Good, you're in charge. Go create a sales department."

Later on, we also needed to expand the client managing and training departments. Patti Lavoie was our top client manager, so I told her to hire a whole group to keep up with our growth. When the need arose because business was so good, we created the departments to handle the volume and continue pushing our growth.

That's how all our departments came into being. On the first day, two or three people handled everything. We were the software department, we were the implementation department. But as the company grew, there weren't enough hours on the face of the earth for us to do it all.

It was a simple process, really. First you get the people, and then when the volume warrants it—when the *sustainable* volume warrants it—you create the departments to continue that growth; otherwise, you can't keep up.

If you create the departments *before* that growth occurs, you saddle yourself with an overhead that can bankrupt your company. When you wait until the revenues are there—not a "spike" increase this week that won't appear again next week, but a steady revenue/profit/cash flow stream—you can afford the expansion with less risk.

A Special Case

It took us six months to train every QSI client manager (CM). The CM had to be a good trainer, a consultant, and a manager, all rolled into one. We could train a trainer in maybe a month, but it took a long time to train the person who helped the client decide what they needed, made sure they received the right system, made sure it was implemented properly, and made sure the trainers did their job properly.

Since I had a six-month lead time before I could hire another client manager, I made sure they were unbelievably busy before I entertained the idea of hiring another one. To me, unbelievably busy means 80 to 100 percent billable time.

If I had thought, "Gee, I'm going to need a lot of these people, I should just go out and hire a bunch of them," I'd have increased my overhead enormously. Instead, I told each new client manager, "I'll pay you bonuses because I know I'm working you really hard." That created another win-win situation: the young CMs had a chance to make a lot of money; the company grew at a reasonable rate without burdening our overhead; the clients got top help from our young, enthusiastic, bonus-driven employees; and the shareholders were happy. Everybody won.

We were careful to bring in people who had already been doing something similar. I primarily hired them from my clients and suppliers, under the honesty code that I would not talk to their people unless they gave me written permission. Under my strict personal code of ethics, I would not talk to anyone without their employer's written consent. If the owner said someone was off limits, I didn't talk to them.

Very often, though, the owner said, "Great! I'd love that person to have a career there."

The surest hire you can get in terms of whether they'll be successful is having seen them work with a customer. So once again, the best hires are the ones by referral—even if it's an in-house referral.

Chapter 25

BUSINESS PLANS

Spell everything out.

Assumptions

One of the key elements of a business plan is the assumptions. Do them by category, such as Employee Expenses:

- Cost of headhunter for five employees = 25 percent of base salary

- Cost of senior programmer number one = $xxx base salary + 30 percent in fringe benefits (social security, insurance, etc.)

Then look at your product assumptions, the things you are selling, the basis for your revenue stream(s) and profits.

- Product one = $xxx each

- Product two = $xxx each

- Number of units of each product sold monthly for the first year and quarterly thereafter

Try to make your assumptions realistic, to the best of your knowledge. Use the Delphi Method: cross-reference your assumptions to see if other people agree they're reasonable.

After you've made assumptions about all your costs and revenues—the basis of your Profit and Loss statements—transform them into spreadsheets that include all the P&L categories going forward. Start with monthly projections, because that's how tightly controlled a new enterprise needs to be. Then you can consolidate those by quarter and finally by years for the next three to five years.

You are projecting not only your sales and costs, you're projecting those three essential elements: Revenue, Profit, and Cash Flow, so model not only your P&L statement but your cash flow on them. Once you've made the assumptions, anybody who is good at spreadsheets can plug the numbers in for you.

Risk Factors

Another key business plan element is Risk Factors. Every risk has two aspects: 1) the probability of it occurring and 2) the impact it will have on your company and your assumptions and projections if it does. Order them from greatest to smallest impact.

Suppose, for example, you assume you'll sell three products a day. There's always the risk that you'll only sell one or two a day. What's the likelihood that will happen, and what will that do to your Revenue/ Profit/Cash Flow projections if it does? Answer: you'll be out of business pretty quickly. Rank this Risk Factor high on the list.

Another example: suppose your sales tax goes up. It might hurt you, but it's not going to kill you. Whether it's likely to happen or not, I'd rank this risk pretty low on the list.

You might not worry about a catastrophic risk if you know the chances of it happening are one in a million. On the other hand, if you know the chances of something are closer to 50 percent, you have to weigh that against its potential effect, and add the next component of the business plan: how you're going to mitigate the risk factors.

Suppose you want to hire five part-time customer service people, but there's a risk they won't be able to handle all the calls. You might over-hire to mitigate not having enough people.

You also need a section in your business plan on Competition and why what you're doing is better than what anyone else is doing. That goes back, once again, to having a win-win-win culture of excellence and only selling the best: if someone buys your product or service, it's because they're better off buying from you than not buying at all, and they're better off buying from you than buying from anyone else. Defining your competitive edge is simply a matter of explaining why this is true.

Address the size of your market in your business plan. How big is it? How big do you want to grow in it? What is the competitive landscape; i.e., what are you competing against now, and what do you anticipate will come out of the woodwork that you don't see now: copy cats of yours and other companies' products?

Another item to include in your plan is how you can make yourself unique and not copy-able, so no one else can lift your ideas and put you out of business. In other words, what is it about your product(s), service(s), or company that mitigates the risk of being replicated?

It's an Evolution

Don't think that just because you've written your business plan—and you need to do it, not someone else—you can put it on the shelf and forget about it. Critique it. Run it again. It's not only a repetitive process, it's an ongoing process. You'll want to dust it off every month or so and say, "Now that I'm in business, how did I do relative to the business plan?" Maybe you'll want to change some things now that you know more from having been on the street, so to speak, for a month, or two, or five. What did you assume that was wrong? And what should you be doing now, rather than what you originally conceived? Should you stay the course, or should you make some changes?

Reviewing your plan every month or few months will throw in your face the glaring errors you omitted or assumptions that were incorrect. They'll jump right off the page if you continually monitor your business from your plan. That can be good or bad, but it will always be clarifying. Suppose you thought you'd only sell three cappuccinos a week, but you're actually selling a thousand. Wow, maybe you should orient your business toward cappuccinos!

That goes back, once again, to being able to admit you made a mistake and being flexible enough to correct it. Flexibility is huge, huge, huge.

Then again, you need to be flexible without being wishy-washy. Wishy-washy means you change your idea every day: I said this today; tomorrow I'll say something different. Flexibility needs to be tempered with focus and commitment.

Keep It Simple

A friend wanted my opinion on a new company and brought the principals in to meet me. They were all from ZeroGravity, the company that did hyperbolic space flights here in the U.S. We talked about their projected business of training people who want to take space flights, like the commercial ones Virgin Galactic plans to offer. In fact, they thought they'd get business from Virgin Galactic.

I said, "Why would they give you that business?"

One of the principals said, "Because they're having a hard time getting funding, and the training infrastructure is a big cost. The owner might gladly give that to us."

That was a great answer: it turned the idea into a positive for Virgin Galactic rather than a negative. "I wouldn't offer you a deal that I wouldn't take myself." You have to look at your business from that perspective.

As the conversation continued, I learned they had paid a company to create a 171-page business plan for them. By the time we finished talking, some two or three hours later, we had put the whole business—the perspective, the ten product lines, the risk factors, the revenue and profit assumptions, and how everything would come together—on a few small pieces of paper. Everything. The whole company on a few 5 x 7 sheets. They were flabbergasted, but I knew the secret: address the important questions, and simplify.

Chapter 26

RIGHT/WRONG PATH DECISIONS

The downside of rapid growth can be loss of control. Don't let that happen.

If you take on one or more partners—and investment capitalists are a type of partner—make sure you maintain 51 percent control of your company. You never want to lose that control. Never. The only person I've ever heard of who regained control after losing it was Steve Jobs, and as I said at the outset of this book, he was one of a kind. No one else can be Steve Jobs, so hold onto a majority percentage of your company—generally considered 51 percent—at all costs.

As the person who controls the company, you are responsible for keeping it on the right path, which means making the right decisions—and just as important, not making bad moves. Some of my experiences with David Wyle, the CEO of SurePrep, come to mind as a good example of both.

David founded two wonderful companies. He would call me to discuss decisions that, had they been implemented, could have taken his whole company down. They were completely non-beneficial, but he was too close to the situation to see that perspective.

Entrepreneurs: Find a Mentor or Coach

You're the one making all the decisions, right or wrong. Your decisions can propel the company to greatness or topple it like a house of straw. With all that riding on your shoulders, you need someone to talk to—either someone in the company you trust wholeheartedly, someone outside the company you can trust, or both.

You need to be able to pick up the phone and say, "Hey, I have to make this tough decision. Can you give me your thoughts and talk with me about the pluses and minuses of this matter?"

The good news about being an entrepreneur is that is you're the boss; the bad news is you're the boss. All the decisions are yours—that's good. On the other hand, you're responsible for every one of them, so try to get as many opinions as you can, especially when you're making key directional decisions for the company.

In David's case, having someone outside his company that he could talk to made the difference between building a successful company he could sell for megabucks and being bankrupt.

Find someone to talk to.

Chapter 27

NEGOTIATIONS & CONTRACTS

Simplicity is key to handling complexities.

When it comes to money and agreements, I believe in being succinct but explicit. I don't want a lot of extra words, and I don't want either party to walk away with any questions or doubts about what we're doing.

Contracts

One: leave no room for ambiguities. If you read a QSI contract, you'll see there's nothing vague or uncertain about it. If there's something in your contract that could be misinterpreted, put in an example so it can't be.

Two: put in anything you promise your client in that contract. Include the definition of anything that costs you a penny or more. I tell my customers, "Anything you want in a contract is in there."

Three: allow no open-ended liability. Don't use any clause that, even in the wildest of possibilities, could bankrupt the company.

Negotiations

Create two columns of issues, one for the money issues and one for the non-money issues. Order them from the highest cost, to the next largest, to the next largest, and so forth.

Do the same thing with the non-money issues, such as the venue's location. Make sure you understand as a business person where the real money is in the contract. "I'll give you eight items that are a dollar, but I'll keep the one that's $100." That's something you can only do by viewing everything as a separate item and analyzing each one's relative importance.

A lot of salesmen make a mistake: they won't discuss deal breakers. It may be contrary to your thinking but you'll arrive at a contract sooner if you tell the other party, "That item is a red line. I'm never going to sign that." You're not being harsh; you're shortening the negotiations.

In any contract negotiation, the other party has to finally tell you what he really wants. He has to. He can't fake it, and he can't hide it. It must come out in the negotiation, or the two of you cannot come to an equitable agreement.

You want to save a lot of money? Agree to your deal points before the lawyers get involved. This is so important. Write out the essentials of the deal you both agree on—what's important to you, what's important to the other side—before you bring in the attorneys. It will keep you from sending endless contract revisions back and forth.

One final point: make sure the other party knows the difference between a legal decision and a business decision. You don't want a lawyer to get involved in making business decisions. That's between you and the other party.

Chapter 28

OUTSIDE VENDORS: ACCOUNTANTS AND ATTORNEYS

Get it in writing from the people who want to put it in writing for you.

I don't like spending a lot of money on lawyers and accountants, so I've developed some cost-cutting practices for working with them. For example, when we first sit down, I ask for a set of assumptions for the project.

"Who's going to work on this? What's his title? Okay, you're John Jones, senior litigator. What's your hourly rate? $xxx. Fine. Who else is going to work on this?"

I also want to know all the phases they'll go through on this project from beginning to completion. In fact, I expect their set of assumptions and budget to cover all professional services, billable hours, rates—everything. And I want it written compactly with SR for Shelly Razin and a legend of everyone else's initials so I can see at a glance who all the players are and what each one charges per hour. I also want to know all the expenses they expect to incur on my behalf. If they're going to hire an expert witness, I want to know who the expert is and how much their testimony or report will cost.

One of the written assumptions from my side of the table is the expectation that I be billed no less than monthly. I'm not interested in waiting a year to receive an enormous, pages-long statement. As the bills come in, I'm going to track them to the budget they've drawn up, so if there's any discrepancy between their written set of assumptions and my bills, I'll know it immediately.

This set of assumptions lays the foundation for our relationship throughout the project. Even so, the first thing most lawyers say is, "Well, I can't really guarantee these charges because sometimes things happen. Unforeseen events occur. That's just the way it is."

I say, "Good! Excellent! As soon as something changes, pick up the phone and tell me what's different. Then give me my new budget."

This approach has significantly reduced my outside services costs over the years.

Ever Vigilant

I never allow my outside service providers to double charge by bringing multiple people to a meeting when you only need to talk to one. That tactic is called "piling on charges," and the people I work with know better. I don't mind that other people are working on my job, but when we have meetings, I expect my primary contact to have all the information in his hands. I'm not interested in spending twice the hourly charge just so a second person can sit in the room.

One way to get the most out of accountants and lawyers is to ask them questions while they're consulting for you. "Hey, can you look at this problem? This is what I think it is; can you critique it?" You're on the phone with them, getting 100 percent of their mind value and all their experience; this is getting true value for their hourly rate.

Remember, you are the decision maker: not your accountant, not your lawyer, not even your doctor. The final decision is yours. Do not ever, ever, abrogate that responsibility. You might want to say, "I did it because my lawyer said to," but you'd only be lying to yourself. Remember, the good news is you're the boss; the bad news is you're the boss. It's your choice. They are only your advisors.

You make the final decision.

With that in mind, if you want to get the most out of meetings, do you homework ahead of time. Don't play it by ear; walk in with a list of your questions, agenda, and goals. Know what you want to achieve by the end of the meeting. That way, you'll both get optimum use of your meeting time.

The same goes for the reverse situation. If your accountant or attorney wants a meeting with you, ask for their questions, agenda, and goals beforehand or at least at the start of the meeting. This will make your time together extremely efficient, and will force you both to think about what you want.

Chapter 29

GOING PUBLIC

Getting off the Treadmill, Part 1

We started Quality Systems in 1973 and incorporated in April 1974. Jump ahead to almost ten years later, and we had built some value. We had our flagship dental turnkey products humming, but we were still living hand-to-mouth.

It's like being on a treadmill. You go in every year and try to get off the treadmill, but no matter how hard you work or how much you make, you never quite get there. As Johnny Carson once quipped, expenses always grow to meet or exceed your income.

When you're in that kind of a situation, you have three choices:

1) Stay on the treadmill

2) Sell your company to a private firm

3) Take the company public

They all have different characteristics.

When you stay on the treadmill, with no outside investors or buyers, you retain super control over the company and its destiny. On the other hand, you're still on the treadmill, working many long hours to just keep your head above water while you keep trying to grow the company. A healthy business must continually grow its revenues and profits.

A lot of people stay on the treadmill because no buyer will offer a reasonable price for the business. You may be too big a force in the company; it may be too dependent on you, a single individual, rather than operate as a company with products.

Then again, you might want to keep the company because you'd rather make your exit at $10 million rather than at a $2 million valuation, and you think that change might be just two or three years away.

In my case, I decided to get off the treadmill and take QSI public after about ten years.

Deciding to take the company public was interesting. There I was, a technical/managerial person running a software company. One day, Graeme Frehner came into my office with a prospectus for AG Software. A broker from his church had given it to him to consider. Graeme handed it to me.

"Shelly, what do you think? Should I invest in this thing?"

I'd never seen a prospectus before. I read it and said, "Wow, these guys bought the shares of their company for pennies and are now selling it to the public for $15 or $17 a share."

Basically, when AG Software went public, the company received a large chunk of money, which meant it had the funds to grow. Just like that, the company wasn't on the treadmill anymore. Plus, the principals also received a large chunk of money, so they could stop worrying about their own personal futures. They were solidified by the money they received from the public offering.

I looked at Graeme. "Shoot, we've got a better company than that! I want to do what they did."

Three underwriters who participated in the AG Software offering were listed on the back of the prospectus. I called each brokerage firm and said, "Hey, look at me, I have a company!"

At that time, we were doubling our sales every year, but we were still a small company. We were about $5.5 million in sales. The only one who answered me was George Bristol from Prudential Bache. He said, "I'll come down and look at your company."

I liked George instantly. He later became a lifelong friend and a member of our board of directors, but I liked him instantly because he was a "street-smart Harvard MBA." That's what I called him.

He said, "Shelly, you're too small right now, but if you do what your projections are telling me—you're going to double again this year—then when the markets open up, you'll be a candidate for us to take public. I'd like to come down every month and monitor how you're doing."

Somewhere around August 1982, he came down and said, "Guess what? Our market experts say we can take your company public."

I said, "Okay. What do we have to do?"

He said, "You're growing nicely, it looks like you'll hit your numbers. The market is getting more receptive to Initial Public Offerings (IPOs) right now. But Shelly, you have no organization. You're the president but you don't have any managers or vice presidents or anything like that under you. You don't even have an accounting firm."

True: Tom Neeson, an extremely competent lifelong friend, did my books.

"You don't have a prestigious law firm, either," George went on. "We'd like you to cure all that."

So that day I went down the aisles and said, "Abe LaLande, you're vice president of hardware. Graeme, you're vice president of software. Grant, you're vice-president of sales and marketing."

I appointed a slew of vice presidents that day, basically creating the kind of organization people on Wall Street wanted to see when they looked at buying into a firm. And I didn't just create the organizational plan; I handed out lists of responsibilities for each position. Now, rather than everything being me-me-me, we had people legitimately in place to run different aspects of the company.

It was as if we were suddenly all grown up.

We hired Price Waterhouse, one of the Big Eight accounting firms of that era, to handle our books. Then we went looking for legal firms. In the end, it came down to two prestigious companies: Gibson, Dunne, and Crutcher or O'Melveny and Myers.

O'Melveny and Myers had an Orange County office because Orange County was starting to boom at that time, but the attorney who showed up to talk to us came down from the Los Angeles office. I didn't know that Warren Christopher would later become Secretary of State under Bill Clinton. I only knew that he was a very nice guy who convinced me to go with O'Melveny.

Actually, as with many either/or situations, O'Melveny didn't win our business as much as Gibson lost it.

We were in September, and I wanted to do the offering as fast as I could. I was aiming for the beginning of December, a mere two months away. I asked each company, "How long will it take you to put this together?"

Gibson, Dunne and Crutcher said it would take maybe six months. So Warren Christopher committed to doing it by the beginning of December. O'Melveny won our business because Gibson lost it.

I'd never gone public, so didn't know anything about the process. The one thing I did know was that we had to write a prospectus. Price Waterhouse said, "We'll help you and your legal people do the prospectus." They had a road map that would take a long time to do, and a lot of my time. So I suggested, "What if I write the prospectus and then you critique it?"

This is the same technique I'd used with lawyers all along. I'd say, "I'll write the contract and then you critique it."

I said, "I know my business, so it's probably easier for me to learn what I need to know from you than it would be for you to learn what you need to know from me."

Price Waterhouse's immediate reaction was to give me a stack of accounting books three feet high. I said, "No, no, no. That's not going to do me any good."

They said, "What do you want?"

I said, "Give me prospectuses of similar companies that have gone public in the last year. I'll look at those."

I closeted myself in the office with those prospectuses, my then controller Brian Schmidt, and my administrative assistant and secretary, Dorothy Sebade, for the weekend. Dorothy said her fingers hurt from banging the keys, but we wrote the whole prospectus in one sweep.

Someone asked, "How did you do that?"

It was very simple. I looked at those official prospectuses as the fraternities' quiz answers. We used them as templates.

"They've got a paragraph here on this subject matter. What can we say about that?"

We cut and pasted the whole thing together. We used the boilerplate statements that pertained to our company. We pieced the whole prospectus together in one weekend.

I saved a copy of what I wrote in our original and what was finally produced after two months of the professionals regurgitating it. They were nearly identical. Most people would not be able tell the difference.

You may ask: why would they play with it for two months?

My answer: going through a public offering is like throwing a wedding or bar mitzvah. The participants are the people you hire for the affair: the caterer, the entertainment, and the photographer. They make their living providing services to people who throw affairs.

For the public offering, you hire accountants and a legal firm. They make their money on the amount of work they put into your prospectus. They'd given us a quote, and they were going to work to those numbers and make that much out of the offering no matter what. At one point after I gave them my prospectus, some eight to twelve people—lawyers and accountants—went back and forth debating whether to use the word shareholder or stockholder.

That one item cost us $20,000.

But you have to look at it in a different framework. When you take a company public, a defined set of people are going to take a cut of the offering. The underwriters take so much percent. The lawyers take their cut. And the accountants take their cut.

If you ask them, the accountants and lawyers will claim they take such heavy cuts because they have a liability in case anybody gets sued. They have to be extremely careful, and that kind of care costs money.

The way I look at it, it was simply the vigorish of the game. Vigorish, or the vig, as gamblers put it, is just what you have to pay somebody to get it done. The money we put out was the vigorish we paid our underwriters, lawyers, and accountants. We also paid the firm that printed the prospectus. It was just the cost of doing business.

In the end, we raised roughly $11 million—in 1982 dollars. That would be equivalent to $19 or $20 million today.

It was a relatively small amount, but it gave the company roughly $5.5 million, and my partners and me about $5.5 million. I personally came away with a very healthy chunk of change, on which, of course, I had to pay taxes, including long-term capital gain because I had founder's stock.

Was it worth it?

I remember when they handed me my check. It was inconceivable I could hold this much money in my hand. I felt like I was in Fantasyland.

Some Things are Negotiable; Some Things are Not

You can negotiate certain elements with your underwriters: the sale price of the stock, for example, the number of insider-shares sales they'll allow, and at what price they value the company. Those are three key elements which are all negotiable.

Some of our clients called to ask for some of the offering. Those people who are given the ability to buy the offering are generally in a position to reap a lot of economic benefit. We originally planned to go out at $17 a share, but the Prudential Bache people called me into their office the day of the offering.

"We have two issues," they said. "Massachusetts won't allow us to use that price. Your mother won't be able to buy any stock." Some states have "blue sky" laws that require you to get approval to sell your stock in their state.

I said, "I don't care if we sell in Massachusetts or not."

They finally allowed the sale, but they wanted to reduce our price from $17 to $15.

I was on pins and needles right up until the day of the offering, but George gave me some good advice. He said, "Stay firm. Don't cave."

So I didn't, and the offering was quite successful. Shortly thereafter, the shares shot from $17 to as high as $45 a share. We split the stock.

Everything Changes

Once you're a public company, you're under public scrutiny. If your stock goes down, you can get sued even if you have done absolutely nothing wrong. Being a publicly traded company comes with added costs and added risk for the shareholders, the directors, and the company's executives that don't exist in a private company.

On the other hand, now that the company was off the treadmill, we didn't have to wait to make some investments if I wanted to. Plus, I was personally off the treadmill. I remember thinking that no matter what happened now, even if things went badly, I had enough money to live on for the rest of my life. I liked that security.

Of course, I still had a stake in the game. I not only had the money I took out of the offering, I also had stock that could appreciate in value. We've had a lot of ups and downs over the decades, but we've split sixteen ways since then, and the value of the company at the beginning of 2014 was more than a billion dollars, so we're riding the value.

That's the public game.

Fill Your Board

Since, again, this was all brand new to me, I went about asking people to sit on the board the same way I looked for talented employees. I looked to the people I already admired and respected.

I started with George Bristol. "Would you do me a favor and be on my board?" He consented. One down, four to go.

My wife Janet was our CFO at the time. That was number two.

We had a lifelong friend, Gordon Setran, who created a savings and loan business on the same street as us, Pinecrest Drive in Corona. Having him on the board gave us a financial expert.

Number three.

George suggested Norman Dreyfuss, who was involved in Marquest Medical, a healthcare products company. That gave us someone else who understood the healthcare business, as well as a celebrity relative: Norman's son Richard had recently won a Best Actor academy award for his role in *The Goodbye Girl*.

With Graeme and me, we had a very collegial board of six. It was a pleasant board to be part of.

That's my story about going public. Now let me give you an alternate way to get off the treadmill.

Chapter 30

SELL YOUR COMPANY

Getting off the Treadmill, Part 2

I worked with Henry Wyle, a computer hardware designer, at Autonetics Rockwell. We'd been friends all those years. His son David, a CPA with Coopers and Lybrand, sat in a Jacuzzi one day in 1996 and talked to me about an idea for an electronic audit for the accounting field. His idea sounded exactly like what we were doing with electronic medical records.

I said, "Why don't you write a business plan?"

He said, "What's a business plan?"

I said, "I'll help you write it."

So we put together a business plan that needed some money, and

I funded $200,000 of the original $250,000 investment. We grew that business, ePace!, very successfully.

One day, we had an offer from CCH, a Chicago-based division of Wolters Kluwer, which was headquartered in Europe. David came to me and said, "They offered to buy our company; what should we do?"

I looked at the offer and even though I had veto power, I said, "I'll do whatever you want, but let me share something with you. The longer you stay with it, the more valuable the company will be."

"On the other hand, Shelly," David pointed out, "you live in a beautiful house on the beach in Laguna and I'm eating peanut butter and jelly. If I had my druthers, I'd like to sell the company."

I couldn't object. Selling is a legitimate alternative for an entrepreneur. David had purposely formed a relationship with CCH knowing they could be a potential buyer one day. He'd been on his company's treadmill at that point for over four years, and although the company had its strengths, he was still living from hand to mouth. He wanted to take advantage of the exit plan he'd been preparing for himself all that time.

When David sold ePace! for around $14 million, roughly $3 million more than QSI got when we went public, I got about 42 percent of it, he got about 31 percent of it, and the other employees and shareholders got the rest. David and I were not satisfied, however, that some of the late-stage investors earned only a 5 percent return on their investment. We discussed the situation and determined no ePace! investor should earn less than a 25 percent annualized return. So David and I reduced our share of the sale proceeds so that these investors would earn that minimum return.

Now that's showing real appreciation for your investors![1]

For David, the upside was getting a significant sum of money and the freedom to look for a second venture. He had to work for them for a year, which is standard, because they needed that for continuity. But he had no responsibilities after that.

When you sell to a private party, there's no public scrutiny. You take your money and you're gone. The other person now owns the company and you are free to do something new. It's a clean slate.

I was later told that ePace!'s product became CCH Software Division's second-best-selling product ever after their tax software, so I have no remorse about it. I always want the other fellow to get a good deal, and he did. Before the final sale went through, I cautioned David, "You're going to get a windfall. I suggest you put it into a house so you can't spend it or gamble it away."

He listened to me and bought a substantial house in Crystal Cove.

One Last Story

David had a contract with CCH to work for them for a year. During that time, he kept calling me to do other companies with him. A lot of them were not in his field, so I said no.

Finally, he had an idea from an ePace! customer, a significant New York accounting firm called Anchin, Block & Anchin, also known as ABA, now called Anchin. They were selling a tax service product that was outsourced to India. I told David, "The reason I like this business is that it's technology-based, it's selling to the same clientele you sold the ePace! products to, and your background fits with this kind of

1. See appendix for complete payout breakdown.

thing. You'll be selling a new product to the same kind of customers as before."

I actually went with him to New York to talk with the ABA people. Then we went to Central Park, and in that one afternoon, we mapped out what this company would be like and how he would do it. Our version was different from what ABA envisioned, but they liked it enough to want a 50/50 partnership. So we formed SurePrep as a 50/50 partnership with Anchin, Block & Anchin.

Eventually, the company needed $3 million more to operate, but ABA didn't want to put in any more capital. I said, "Okay, I'll be the anchor, I'll guarantee the shares so we get all the money we need. Even if the current shareholders only buy one share, I'll buy all the rest. But I want to be fair, so any shareholder can buy the shares at the same price I'm buying them."

ABA didn't buy anything. They dropped out; they didn't want anything to do with it. Some of the other people who had owned shares in the original company put up more money, which came to about 5 percent. As a result, I wound up with 95 percent of the new shares.

The choices I made throughout my career are what put me in the position to be able to personally bail out a multi-million-dollar company. How many people can say that?

If you are cut from this entrepreneurial cloth; if you want to make your path rather follow someone else's; if you get a thrill out of watching something grow as a result of your ingenuity and are willing to take the risks and put in the time necessary to create your own financial security out of nothing—then perhaps you are destined to tell a story or two of your own one day.

Make the choice. Step on the path.

31 SIMPLE BUT ELEGANT

Reports

Everything should be able to be put on an 8 ½ by 11 with exhibits and the assumptions used

- Sales Reports
- Customer Service Reports
- Client Management Reports
- Customer Training Reports
- Software Development Project Formats
- Division Heads' Goals
- Human Resource Duties
- Project Billing Update Reports
- Investment Criteria

Sales Reports

Each sales person should provide the following type of reporting at least on a monthly basis.

Sort by sales close date

Sales Person	Brent Underwood (BU)
Four-week forecast:	Jones Medical (JM) $300K 10-1-14 Saint Mary's (SM) $450K 10-18-14 Total 4 week forecast: $750K
Forecast for rest of year:	Wheeler Medical (WM) $800K 11-12-14 Johnson Anesthesia (JA) $1.2M 12-23-14
Near-term closes	
What changed to make them buy now:	JM-Priority of new leadership SM-Etc.
Decision maker(s):	JM-Jimmy Jones (JJ), CEO
Decision influencer(s):	JM-Barry Miller (BM), CFO JM-Les Miner (LM), CIO
Timeline to close:	See above
Possible obstacles to close:	JM-Contractual negotiations involving legal counsel
Plan to mitigate risk of not closing:	JM-Make sure we have a signed off term sheet before going to legal
Your strategy to close the deal:	JM-Involve the new CEO to back the term sheet.

The sales manager should have a consolidated report of all sales people and should update this report monthly.

October	$1.55M	BU: $750K (JM-$300K; SM-$450K)
		HG: $800K (KS-$250K; WA-$550K)
November	$1.78M	BU: $800K (WM-$800K)
		HG: $980K (TG-$430K; KP-$550K)
Dec	$1.25M	BU: $1.20M (JA-$1.2M)
Total	$4.58M	

Customer Service Reports

All reported issues coming from a client need to be recorded and tracked until they're resolved. These reports can be useful in tracking the efficiency of each support representative as well as pointing the way to what other actions should be taken as a result of what was found out on this service call.

Detail per customer

Responsible Support Representative:	David Jones (DJ)
Manifest issue (symptom):	System response time for entering patients is too slow.
How did we find the real issue:	Testing the client's bandwidth revealed the source of the problem.
Real issue:	As the client staff grew the bandwidth became insufficient.
Was this problem called in before:	___ yes _x_ no
What was done to fix problem:	The client contacted their ISP and increased their bandwidth.
What changed after the fix:	Their response time went from 5 seconds to .5 seconds.
What other departments need to take action:	
___ Software Development	
___ Training	
___ Hardware	
___ Documentation	
_x_ Support	Support should monitor clients for these kinds of problems.
___ Client Management	
___ Sales	
___ Legal	
___ Contracts	
Time getting back to customer from call initiation:	20 minutes
Time to fix problem from call initiation:	2 Days

Client Management Reports

Client managers are ultimately responsible for ensuring your product or service is successfully delivered and the client is happy. These people are hard to find because they must not only have consulting and management capability, but they also need to thoroughly know your product and how the client can maximize its use in their setting. They also need to have great intrapersonal and communication skills. In order to do their jobs they need access and command over a team of trainers, software developers (if necessary), and other organizational resources. If they accomplish their stated goals, your clients will be a source of recommendations and referrals. If they don't, you need to understand the issues at hand and the steps being taken to get the client back on track. Client Management Reports like the one below will help you assess whether your client managers are meeting their goals so you can build your customer base.

For software companies

Responsible for overall customer success	Jim Jones (JJ)
Milestone charts and completion dates	See Customer Training Reports; software 3-1-14, data conversion and software parameter selection 3-4-14; hardware installation 2-24-14; implementation sign-off 5-5-14
Customer ratings (on a scale of 1 to 10 with 10 being highest) and detail of things we did good and/or bad:	
Overall customer satisfaction	9-no comments
Client managing satisfaction	9-loved the client manager
Training satisfaction	10-no comments
Product satisfaction	8-Some user interfaces could improve such as the patient portal component
Timeliness	10-no comments
Did we deliver all contractual items? On time? If not, list open items.	9-no open items
Would you recommend us? If not, why not?	Yes

Customer Training Reports

Customer staff should be trained specific to their function. At the start of the training tell them what they'll learn and at the end test them to make sure they learned it. A report like the one below, for each position that needs to be trained, can help make sure you maximize the customer's use of the system.

Course definition:	Training for Front Desk Receptionist
Name/position of trainee:	Sally Jones/Front Desk Receptionist
At end of training, trainee will know how to:	Register a patient; check eligibility; …
Customer tests (administered to each trainee, test scores retained by QSI and are available to be shared with client)	Register Sally Jones as patient (from the attached data sheet) and check her eligibility. Provide a score for her test.
Course Schedule for Sally Jones: *Registering patients and checking eligibility	E-learning course complete by 7/1/14; testing successfully completed by 7/7/14

Make a list of every position type that needs to be trained and what courses they need to pass in what timeframe. The client manager, the person responsible for the client's success, will work with the client to identify the people needing to be trained.

Staff Positions	Staff Names	Course Names	Start Dates	Completion Dates
Front Desk Receptionists	Sally Jones	Course #1	6/20/14	7/7/14
	John Smith	Course #1	6/20/14	7/7/14
System Administrators	Norah Bentley	Course #1, Course #2, Course #6	6/21/14	7/8/14
	Jimmy Black		6/21/14	7/8/14
Etc.				

The entire implementation project should be summarized in a timeline chart including all the major milestones.

Software Development Project Formats

Software development reports allow you to review the budgets, milestones, and staff assignments for all projects at a single glance.

PRODUCT	BH	P-T-D	RH	CCD	B	GR	ACD	ACM	CC
								AS OF DATE: 02/28/	
DENTAL									
DU	10,400	1,657	8,743	05/14/14	06/01/14	07/16/14	400,400	171,600	SP, FF, JS
QDW	33,280	5,303	27,977	05/14/14	06/01/14	03/23/14	964,608	321,536	SP, FF, K\
EDR	17,160	2,734	14,426	02/01/14	03/15/14	05/31/14	380,812	101,228	SP, FF, JS
MIRTH									
MR	43,680	6,960	36,720	07/01/14	08/01/14	09/30/14	1,768,016	442,004	SP, JT, GI
MC	17,097	3,646	13,451	07/01/14	08/01/14	09/30/14	660,261	165,065	SP, JU, W
MM	7,771	1,657	6,114	07/01/14	08/01/14	09/30/14	249,929	62,482	JT, GB, N
MMA	4,663	994	3,669	07/01/14	08/01/14	09/30/14	205,166	51,291	GB,MM
MCR	17,097	3,646	13,451	07/01/14	08/01/14	09/30/14	522,240	130,560	SP, JT, SQ
*NGHS									
HSC	34,320	668	33,652	01/15/14	02/10/14	03/06/14	1,350,960	900,640	SP, CG/K\
HSF	32,240	5,137	27,103	02/28/14	04/15/14	05/15/14	731,480	1,097,220	SP, CG/K
NGRx	7,280	1,160	3,120	02/03/14	04/14/14	05/15/14	200,200	200,200	SP, CG/K\
SURG	6,760	1,077	5,683	n/a	n/a	n/a	185,900	185,900	SP, CG/K\
HSS	-	2,071	(2,071)	02/10/14	04/15/14	05/15/14	-	-	SP, CG/K\
EDD	13,000	2,071	10,929	02/10/14	04/15/14	05/15/14	357,500	357,500	SP, CG/K\
LAB	9,360	1,491	7,869	05/01/14	08/01/14	01/21/14	257,400	257,400	SP, CG/K\
HSKBM	11,440	1,823	9,617	02/14/14	02/14/14	03/06/14	-	629,200	SP, CG/K\
INX	5,200	829	4,371	n/a	n/a	n/a	-	286,000	SP, CG/K\
NGA									
PM	210,080	33,474	176,606	01/17/14	02/28/14	04/14/14	3,998,250	3,998,250	SP, TE, RI
HER	122,720	19,554	103,166	01/17/14	02/28/14	04/14/14	4,043,562	695,708	SP, TE
KBM	272,480	43,417	229,063	n/a	n/a	03/01/15	7,189,378	4,792,918	SP, TE
OP	4,160	663	3,497	01/17/14	02/28/14	04/14/14	114,400	114,400	SP, BD, DI

The legend for the column labels should be provided on another page such as the one below.

Item	Description
Product	Product or development project
BH	Budgeted Hours: Total budgeted hours for each product for one year based on current FTE staffing levels
P-T-D	Progress-To-Date: The number of hours used for the product so far this year as of the date at the top of the page
RH	Remaining Hours: The total Budgeted Hours less number of hours in the Progress To Date
CCD	Code Complete Date: Date new feature will be fully coded product can be given to clients in a non-production environment
BD	Beta Date: The date the product will become available to a small set of customers for beta testing in a production environment
GR	General Release: The date the product will be available to all clients for upgrade
ACD	Annual Cost to Develop: Annualized projected cost to develop based on salary cost of R&D div & other exp using new dev % of total costs
ACM	Annual Cost to Maintain: Est annualized cost of salaries & stated exp in R&D div required to maintain software 1 yr, using maint % of the total
CC	Chain of Command: The people in the organization who have responsibility for the success of the project

The legend for the staff will similarly be provided on another page such as the one below.

Code	Employee Name	Division	Reports To	Reports To
AC	Ana Croxton	EDI	Donn Neufeld	Dan Morefield
AT	Andy Thorson	Mirth	Gerad Brotis	Jon Teichrow
BD	Ben Dubinsky	NGA	Tim Eggena	Tim Eggena
BP	Billy Parish	NG7	Robert Hale	Ben Mehling

For each product listed in the summary report shown on the previous page a more detailed report should be provided that describes an overview of the project, a description of the functionality being developed, an overview of the competition and the product's competitive advantages, the business model, financial projections, and so on.

Product Information				Pricing & Projections					
Name: Dental Web		**Chain of Command:** SW, FF, RA, RB		**Price Model:**					
Mnemonic: QDW		**Code Complete Date:** 02/28/14		1. Subscription: ~$75 per user per month list (down to $28)					
Internal Name: Dental Web		**Beta:** 03/23/14							
Version: 2.0		**General Release:** 03/23/14		**Projections (000s):**					
Product Overview						Q1	Q2	Q3	Q4
Provides unparalleled access to info needed to increase revenue, decrease costs and maximize efficiency. This next big advance in web-based solutions allows you to be in touch and in control anytime and anywhere your web-enabled device can be accessed. This innovative technology offers integrated all-in-one clinical admin data management for your practice by making it easier to access and view patient records, digital charting, and patient data.				FY15	Sales	350	350	350	350
				FY15	Maint	325	325	325	325
				FY16	Sales	588	588	588	588
				FY16	Maint	1,125	1,125	1,125	1,125
Functionality		**Competition**		FY17	Sales	688	688	688	688
All aspects of managing large practices		Cuve		FY17	Maint	1,750	1,750	1,750	1,750
Graphical charting		Dentrix Cloud Product						Total	1
Treatment plans		Denticon							
Easy-to-use forms				**Budget**					
Voice-activated perio charting									
Online patient registration				**FTEs**	**Cnt**	**Wks**	**Hours**	**RT**	T
Supports chartless or paperless office		.		US	5	52	10,400	$55	$
Highly optimized/customizable flow				India	11	52	22,880	$18	$
EDI services (statements, claims, reminders, etc)				**Travel**	**Cnt**		**Cost**		T
Buyers		**Competitive Advantage**		US	0		$1,500		
Dental practices with 3+ providers		SaaS model; cloud based - dozens of advantages		US/India	0		$8,000		
Dental Practices with 2+ locations		Easy to implement and use		**Licenses**	**Cnt**		**Cost**		T
Dental practices of all sizes		Minimal up-front investment to begin using			0		$0		
Organization with multiple offices		Can scale quickly to accommodate growth			0		$0		
Multi-specialty dental practices		Enterprise management solution		**Other**	**Cnt**	**Note**	**Cost**		T
		Web-enabled device access		Independent Contr	1	EDI	$57,204		$
				Aloha MU2/3	1		$245,100		$
Limitations		**Competitive Disadvantage**		**TOTAL DEVELOPMENT COST**					$1,
Reliant on decent office internet connection		Services (conversion, training, etc) are expensive		75% of total for new development					$
				25% of total for new maintenance					$
				% US Resources: 31%		**% India Resources:**			

Notes	
Item	**Note**
Projections	Sales Projections include new subscriptions and services; Maint Inc annual subscriptions and EDI revenue. (annual numbers provided were divided evenly into
Budget	Development costs rep product rather than project. Calculated by taking the total number of R&D FTEs and using 75% (12) for new dev and 25% (4) for maint.
Budget	All expenses shown are budget projections that have not been reviewed and approved

Version Control			
Ver	**Date**	**Author**	**Description**
1	03/06/14	DP	Created original Document.
2	03/15/14	DP	Made format changes and added information provided by JT

Division Heads' Goals (All Heads' Common Goals)

What do you want from your division heads? What are their most important goals? Ranking their progress on a scale of 1 to 10 (10 being best) on goals such as the ones below is a simple way to evaluate their performance.

Meet or exceed Revenues/Profits/Cash Flow per [year] budget	10
Customer satisfaction is 90%+	9.5
Employee performance & morale excellent	9.5
Key new people hired and are winners	8
Working in collaboration with other business units	7.5
Innovative performance achieved	7
Develop succession people at all levels	5
Acquisitions success + acquisitions made	4
New business partners acquired and are a success	4

Each division head should give you a self-performance review on each of these areas with backup substantiation on a monthly basis. And if he's not meeting the desired goals what is his plan for improvement?

Human Resources Duties

Having a high performing HR department is critical to the success of your business. If you don't have the resources you need you won't be able to properly execute on opportunities. Make sure your HR director provides the bandwidth necessary for growth by setting appropriate goals such as the ones below.

1. Help hire personnel at minimum cost and with minimum use of headhunters who are successful after six months on the job

2. Develop succession plans across the organization

3. Identify key people and create development plan to help them grow

4. Identify personnel earning over $100k who are either under or overpaid. Make appropriate recommendations

5. Get all divisions on the same HR benefits and other plans

6. Assess operations in all locations with respect to pay and HR. Make appropriate recommendations

7. Provide monthly reports to the compensation committee chairman on all of the above

8. Rank all personnel from most valuable to least valuable along with their compensation to determine who is underpaid/overpaid and what action, if any, should be taken.

Outside Professional Services Billing Reports

The following reports should be submitted as indicated upon initiation of an outside the company professional service project. This project billing report should be updated monthly and immediately when budget changes occur. Each report should have the Project name/ code, revision number and date prepared.

Project: Default Notice Response (DNR)		
Report #	Name	When Generated
Rpt #1	Billable Staff on Project	On start of project + on any change
Rpt #2	Project Schedule	On start of project + on any change
Rpt #3	Projected Costs	On start of project + on any change
Rpt #4	Budget Change Report	On any budget change(s)
Rpt #5	Monthly Billing Report	Monthly (for each project)

Report Format Samples

Rpt #1: Billable Staff (DNR)   01/02/2010

Project: Default Notice Response (DNR)			
Initial	Rate	Name	Position
TKN	$ 350	Todd K Norman	Partner
JB	$ 250	John Bledsoe	Associate
JD	$ 100	Jane Davison	Paralegal

Rpt #2: Project Milestones/Dates   01/02/2010

Project: Default Notice Response (DNR)	
03/17/10	Initial Assessment
03/20/10	Finalize Plan
03/25/10	Send Notice of Default
04/02/10	Resolve if possible with agreement
04/09/10	File and Serve lawsuit
04/12/10	Draft Settlement agreement to customer
04/15/10	Reach agreement on terms of settlement
04/20/10	Court approval of settlement and dismissal of suit

Rpt #3: Projected Costs (DNR)   01/02/2010

Project: Default Notice Response (DNR)			
(A) Personnel			
Initials	Hrs	Rate	Total
TKN	20	$350	$7,000
JB	15	$250	$3,750
JD	25	$100	$2,500
Total	60		$13,250
(B) Other Costs			
Postage/Express Services:			$200
Filing Fees, etc.:			$850
Total			$1,050
(C) Total Project Costs			
Personnel			$13,500
Other Costs			$1,050
Total			$14,300

Assumptions:

1. AK will not be able to bring action to stop demand note

2. No additional motions filed by McDermott or Razin

3. No separate lawsuit filed by AK or Razin

4. Court does not require a response to counterclaim or motion for summary judgment prior to hearing

5. Court holds a single full-day evidentiary hearing and hears arguments on all pending motions, after which it (a) strikes the filings by McDermott and recognized Norman as counsel for Milestone, and (b) approves the current Settlement Agreement.

Project: Default Notice Response (DNR)						
Project	Rev	Date	Tot$	Per$	Other $	Reason for Change
DNR	R#01	03/10/10	$21,550	$18,500	$3,050	Extra depositions required as of 2/14/10
DNR	Orig	01/02/10	$14,300	$13,250	$1,050	Original budget

(A) Personnel			
Initials	Hrs	Rate	Total
TKN	30	$350	$10,500
JB	20	$250	$5,000
JD	30	$100	$3,000
Total	80		$18,500

(B) Other Costs	
Postage/Express Services:	$200
Filing Fees, etc.:	$850
Travel	$2,000
Total	$3,050

(C) Total Project Costs	
Personnel	$13,500
Other Costs	$1,050
Total	$21,550

Rpt#5: Monthly Billing Report (DNR) Period: 01/01~03/31/2010
02/09/2010

Project: Default Notice Response (DNR)					
(A) Personnel					
	This Period			Cumulative to Date	
Initials	Hrs	Rate	Total	Hrs	Total
TKN	5	$350	$1,750	5	$1,750
JB	6	$250	$1,500	6	$1,500
JD	12	$1,200	$1,200	12	$1,200
Total	23		$4,450	23	$4,450
(B) Other Costs					
			This Period	Cumulative to Date	
Postage/Express Services:			$65	$65	
Filing Fees, etc.:			$150	$150	
Total			$215	$215	
(C) Total Project Costs					
			This Period	Cumulative to Date	
Personnel			$4,450	$4,450	
Other Costs			$215	$215	
Total			$4,665	$4,665	

Investment Criteria

Once you're successful in growing your business you'll have money to invest in other ones (and plenty of people asking for it!). Money is hard to earn and easy to lose. Make sure you vet each personal investment against the criteria below before putting your money at risk. The questions and answers shown below relate to actual investments I have evaluated against these criteria.

1. What is the strategy to be employed (explain in detail)? What has been the track record and for how long? What causes the profit to happen? How much leverage may be used?

   TPS Partners has the opportunity to acquire ABC Apartments, a 544 unit complex in Jackson, Mississippi. The asset will be purchased with new financing up to 80% of purchase price from FNMA at a fixed interest rate for 10 years at 221 bps over the 10 YR UST. The property maintains a current physical occupancy of 92% as of January 31, 2014 and has been historically around this range. The purchase price is $16,500,000, or $30k per unit. Based on the current net operating income, the cap rate on the purchase price is 8.1% and 7.4% on total cost.

2. What is the expected gain % and low-water mark for a day, a week, a month, a year, five years, in both pre-tax and estimated after-tax dollars, and what type of taxation is the investment subject to? (Historical and forward predictions)?

   The leveraged IRR for the property is projected to be 25% (10-year hold). The unlevered IRR is projected to be 14%. The investor IRR is expected to be 22% with a 5.0x equity multiple.

3. Who makes what money out of this deal (how much and when), including fees going in or out (commissions, etc.) as well as ongoing flows (including management or service & maintenance costs associated with the assets, noting those paid to related entities of the manager)?

Preferred return to investors is 8%, then 80% to investors and 20% to TPS after catch-up to TPS. Acquisition fee is 1% of purchase price and improvements; asset management fee is 0.5% of purchase price with 2% annual increases, disposition fee 1.0% of sales price or refinance amount. Additionally, there will be a 1% loan broker fee (probably $140k), a 2.5% annual property management fee (external company) on revenue (about $75k/yr), contractors/companies doing the improvements (~$1 million initially and more in years ~2-4), and a sales broker fee on final sale of ~1-1.25%.

4. What are the risks: detail all and how mitigated by strategy? Order these in order of worst damage and by most expected?

	Risk	*Mitigating Factor*
1	*Re-enter economic downturn and experience rental rate deterioration.*	*• Region/location selection with a very low foreseen probability of impact on rents and significant occupancy reduction (this region has had 2% rent growth on average and no reductions over last 20 years, based on a recent research report).*
2	*Supply of new multifamily projects.*	*• Conservative modeling showing an occupancy reduction to 75% from 92% would still break-even cash-flow (with no 8% payments to investors), so there is staying power.* *• Monitoring and projecting trends in case of a crisis, could attempt to sell before the full impact of the storm (though this would likely be at a discount)*
3	*Tornados or other natural disasters.*	*Insurance*

5. What is the liquidity? If I put in $1 today and sell tomorrow (assume asset prices are unchanged), how much do I get?

    Investors have the right to sell their units to other accredited investors or liquidate the project with a vote of 65% of the Membership Interest. Asset liquidation (while an extreme and unlikely path) would return 97%probably ~86% of initial equity contribution. (After acquisition fee of 3.5% of equity, loan broker fee of 2.8% of equity, sales commission cost of ~4% of equity, other closing costs of ~3.5% of equity, and likely other wind-down costs, including partial year engagement fees for management, etc.) This is close because leverage is now working against you with such a short duration. On an unleveraged basis it would be 96.5%.

6. What is the investment correlated to? Dow? S&P? Asian Markets? Interest rates? US dollar? Euro? Other? List all.

    Apartments assimilate fixed income or specifically high grade corporate bonds. Warren Buffet was recently quoted as saying "We look at each of our investments as being the ownership of a piece of a company with good long term value, similar to owning a farm or an apartment house".

7. How much can I lose before I'm out? Detail Why?

    Our downside scenario assumes 0% rent growth for 10-years, which would yield an 8.1% IRR to investor and a 1.7x equity multiple. Modeling shows that ~86% occupancy at current rent rates is break-even, including debt service (but not including 8% preferred payment to limited members, so no funds would be available for those distributions). In an extreme scenario, since up to 80% leverage is used, the entire amount invested can be lost.

8. Who else has done this? (Other people employing this strategy and customers who have participated in this strategy

Predominately, this market is covered by private investors, but is seeing more institutional presence. AAA Properties, non-traded REIT, located in Newport Beach has been in Jackson since 2012. Starplus reentered the market in 2013.

9. What is the frequency and timeliness (how many days past "as of") of reporting and access (can we get on demand) to information regarding the underlying assets held and their current value?

Investor reporting and distributions will be sent out quarterly.

ABOUT THE AUTHOR

Sheldon Razin [Founder, Chairman, Quality Systems Inc.] is what entrepreneurs dream of: he took $2,000 of his own money and built a company that's now worth $1.4 billion at recent check.
—Orange County Business Journal, March 30-April 5, 2009

Sheldon Razin – Chairman of the Board, Quality Systems, Inc.

Sheldon Razin is the founder of Quality Systems, Inc (QSI) which develops and markets computer-based practice management and electronic health records solutions as well as revenue cycle management applications and connectivity services for medical and dental group practices and hospitals throughout the US. He has served as its Chairman of the Board since the Company's incorporation in 1974 (inception 1973) and served as QSI's Chief Executive Officer from 1974 until April 2000.

Sheldon graduated from the Massachusetts Institute of Technology with a Bachelor's of Science Degree in Mathematics in 1959. Sheldon began his career with the Radio Plane division of Northrop where he did programming and operations research projects. He then went to work for the Autonetics division of North American Aviation, which later merged into Rockwell International. With Rockwell, Sheldon conducted mathematical modeling and operations research simulation for computerized inventory control systems. This led to his consulting with many Rockwell divisional presidents whom he advised on long range computer planning and inventory control procedures and policies. Another major achievement was the design and development of a novel computerized Loran navigation technique which became widely used by the U.S. Navy. Sheldon presented this significant work at an international conference in Paris in 1967.

At the age of 35, Sheldon decided to follow his entrepreneurial dreams of owning his own company by starting Quality Systems. Without any venture capital funding, and financed with a $2,000 investment of his own money, Sheldon built QSI into a public company with a multi-billion dollar market capitalization while remaining debt free.

QSI has been recognized as the one of the best performing stocks on Wall Street, named Forbes magazine's third fastest growing small companies, winner of the American Business Awards' Stevie for Company of the Year in Computer Services and many more. Sheldon has also earned many prestigious awards and achievements throughout the years for his stewardship of QSI including Ernst & Young's Regional Entrepreneur of the Year, Orange County Business Journal's Excellence in Entrepreneurship, and American Business Awards' Chairman of the Year to name a few.

In addition to Sheldon's involvement in QSI, he continues to demonstrate his financial savvy and satisfy his entrepreneurial cravings by providing seed funding, mentoring and guidance as the Chairman of the Board for two successful start-ups. First with ePace! Software, a pioneer in paperless engagement software for accounting firms which sold to CCH, Inc a division of Wolters Kluwer a multi-billion dollar Dutch-based publisher, then with SurePrep, a technology company that provides paperless tax workflow software and services to public accounting firms ranging in size from small local firms to the Big Four.

Sheldon maintains connections to his alma mater, MIT, by serving on the advisory board of the McGovern Brain Institute. He created a $1 million endowed fellowship in support of their research, which has served to meet an anonymous challenge grant of $500,000.

Sheldon Razin now resides in Laguna Beach, California with his wife Janet and enjoys spending quality time with his two children and five grandchildren as well as travelling, sailing, scuba diving, snorkeling, swimming and tennis.

APPENDIX I

Going Public vs. Selling Your Company

As discussed in Chapters 29 and 30, two ways an entrepreneur can 'get off the treadmill' are by going public or selling your company. The tables below show how QSI's public offering and ePace!'s private sale impacted their respective shareholders and provide a good example of the benefits and drawbacks of each approach.

Going Public

We took QSI public nine years after its founding when it had about $10M to $10.5M in sales. One advantage of going public is that it generally provides a higher valuation than a private sale. On the other hand, you can only sell a small portion of your shares and must continue to lead the company for the foreseeable future. If you want to completely cash out and move on then going public is not for you. But if you want to continue growing your company while maintaining a significant stake in it then going public is a great option. In my case, although I cashed out about 16% of my shares I maintained a majority interest in QSI which was worth far more than the shares I sold and whose value would grow, if held, more than 77-fold to over $1.6B at its peak.

QSI's Public Offering on 12/01/1982

Net Dollars					
	SR	GF	GS	QSI	Total
# of Shares	239,267	48,141	2,592	370,000	660,000
$17/share	$4,067,539	$818,397	$44,064	$6,290,000	$11,220,000
Less Underwriter Fee of $1.25/sh	($299,084)	($60,176)	($3,240)	($462,500)	($825,000)
Subtotal	$3,768,455	$758,221	$40,824	$5,827,500	
Less Expenses*	($10,515)	($2,337)	($130)	($282,063)	($295,045)
Subtotal	$3,757,940	$755,884	$40,694	$5,545,437	
Less 25% Taxes	($939,485)	($188,971)	($10,174)	$0	($1,138,630)
Net Proceeds	$2,818,455	$566,913	$30,521	$5,545,437	$8,961,326

Net Worth @ $17/sh and % After Offering					
	SR	GF	GS	QSI	Total
# of shares	1,244,335	277,527	15,059	660,000	2,196,921
@ $17/ share	$21,153,695	$4,717,959	$256,003	$11,220,000	$37,347,657
%	56.64%	12.63%	0.69%	30.04%	100.00%

*Expense Detail	
Legal (O'Melveny & Meyers)	$125,370
Printing Prospectuses (Jeffry's)	$69,937
Accounting (Price Waterhouse)	$44,600
Blue Sky filing	$20,620
Accounting (Tom Neeson)	$16,485
Clerical	$7,730
Road Show Expense	$4,000
Road Show Expense to PW	$3,035
Stock Certificate Printing	$1,868
Postage	$1,400
Total Other Expenses	$295,045

Key	
Sheldon Razin	SR
Graeme Frehner	GF
Grant Sadler	GS
Quality Systems Inc	QSI

Selling Your Company

We sold ePace! four years after its founding when it had about
$1M in sales. The advantage of selling your company outright is
that you completely monetize your shares and have no obligation to
continue with the company (other than for a transition period which
generally is about one year). Although you no longer retain any stake
in the company you started, you are free to pursue other ventures.

ePace! Software's Sale to CCH on 3/16/2001

Net Dollars							
	SR	DW	CY	CCH	INV	OE	Total
# of Shares	3,123,679	2,300,000	600,000	734,909	617,310	27,500	7,403,398
$1.89/share	$5,912,305	$4,353,297	$1,135,643	$1,389,730	$1,168,406	$52,050	$14,011,431
Special Allocation	$ (28,800)	$ (28,800)			$ 57,600		$ -
Subtotal	$5,883,505	$4,324,497	$1,135,643	$1,389,730	$1,226,006	$52,050	
Less Expenses	$ (42,193)	$ (31,067)	$ (8,104)	$ (9,927)	$ (8,338)	$ (371)	$ (100,000)
Net Proceeds	$5,841,312	$4,293,430	$1,127,539	$1,379,803	$1,217,668	$51,679	$13,911,431
%	41.99%	30.86%	8.11%	9.92%	8.75%	0.37%	100.00%

KEY	
Sheldon Razin	SR
David Wyle	DW
Carl Yilunto	CY
CCH	CCH
Investors	INV
Other Employees	OE

Note: CCH had made an investment of $1.4M in ePace! For 10% of the company in May of
2000 and bought the whole company for approximately $14M in February 2001.

APPENDIX II

Quality Systems, Inc. Awards and Honors

Quality Systems' track record of strategic growth, profitability and innovation in the industry are well documented. The following is a partial list of third party recognition that Quality Systems and its leadership team have received for outstanding performance over the last five years.

- June 2014 – **American Business Awards**
  - Company of the Year - Health Products & Services – Gold

- November 2013 – **BestInBiz**
  - Chairman of the Year – Gold

- August 2013 – **International Business Awards**
  - Company of the Year - Computer Services – Gold

- July 23, 2013 – Quality Systems Recognized Winner in a record-breaking[2] Nine Categories of the **Best in Biz Awards 2013** – International Competition:
  - Executive Team of the Year category – Gold
  - Most Innovative Product of the Year category – Gold
  - Small or Medium Business Product of the Year category – Gold
  - Best New Product Feature of the Year category – Gold
  - Finance Executive of the Year category – Silver
  - Legal Executive of the Year category – Silver
  - Technology Executive of the Year category – Silver
  - Support Executive of the Year category – Bronze
  - Event of the Year category – Bronze

- June 25, 2013: Quality Systems Recognized in 12 Categories of **11th Annual American Business Awards**, including awards for:
  - Company of the Year - Health Products & Services – Gold

2. Record-breaking means the highest number of categories/awards a single company has won in Best in Biz Awards 2013 International. 2013 was the inaugural international competition for this program.

- November 8, 2012: Quality Systems Appears on F**orbes' Annual List of America's 100 Best Small Companies** for 12th Consecutive Year

- October 18, 2012: Quality Systems Wins Four Gold Stevie Awards in **2012 9th Annual International Business Awards**, including awards for:
  - Best New Product or Service of the Year, Business-to-Business Products - Quality Systems/NextGen NextPen™
  - 2012 Grand Stevie Award Presented to Quality Systems, Inc. For Top Organization of the Year

- June 18, 2012: Quality Systems Wins 14 Stevie Awards in **10th Annual American Business Awards**, including awards for:
  - Steven T. Plochocki, CEO: Executive of the Year - Health Products & Services
  - Management Team of the Year
  - Company of the Year - Health Products & Services
  - Fastest Growing Tech Company of the Year - Up to 2,500 Employees
  - Most Innovative Tech Company of the Year - Up to 2,500 Employees
  - 2013 Grand Stevie Award Presented to Quality Systems, Inc. For #1 in the Top 10 Placement

- June 22, 2012: Quality Systems Chief Financial Officer Paul A. Holt Named Best Finance Executive in **TechAmerica's 19th Annual High-Tech Innovation Awards**

- June 4, 2012: Quality Systems Included in **Forbes' Annual List of America's 25 Fastest-Growing Tech Companies**

- November 7, 2011: Quality Systems Ranks 14th on **Forbes' Annual List of America's 100 Best Small Companies**

- October 13, 2011: Quality Systems Recognized as a Winner in four categories of the **International Business Awards**, including Company of the Year and IT Executive of the Year

- March 14, 2011: Quality Systems Included in **Forbes' Annual List of America's 25 Fastest-Growing Tech Companies** Ranks 23rd

- March 10, 2011: Quality Systems Chairman of the Board Sheldon Razin Honored as Director of the Year in **16th Annual Forum for Corporate Directors Awards**

- November 18, 2010: Quality Systems Ranks on **Forbes' Annual List of America's Best Small Companies for 10th Consecutive Year**

- October 13, 2010: Quality Systems Chairman of the Board and Founder Sheldon Razin Named Winner in Software Category of **TechAmerica's 52nd Annual Innovator Awards**

- July 28, 2010: Quality Systems' NextDDS Solution Wins **2010 American Business Award**

- April 7, 2010: Quality Systems Included in **Forbes' 2009 List of America's 25 Fastest-Growing Tech Companies** Ranking as 23rd

- October 22, 2009: Quality Systems Ranks Third On **Forbes Annual List of America's 200 Best Small Companies**

- June 29, 2009: Quality Systems Chairman of the Board and Founder Sheldon Razin Wins **2009 American Business Award's "Chairman of the Year" Award**

- June 15, 2009: Quality Systems Chairman of the Board and Founder Sheldon Razin Named **Ernst & Young 2009 Entrepreneur of the Year in Healthcare Category for Orange County/Desert Cities Program**

- March 24, 2009: Quality Systems Chairman Sheldon Razin **Earns Excellence in Entrepreneurship Award from Orange County Business Journal**

- December 1, 2008: Quality Systems Ranks Fourth **On Forbes Annual List of America's 200 Best Small Companies**

INDEX

A

A G. Becker Securities, 17, 18

AG Software, 132, 133

Allen, Paul, 33, 35

Anastasia, 69, 70

Anchin, Block & Anchin (ABA), 143, 144

Apple, 30, 50, 51

Aramco (*also see Saudi Arabian Oil*), 22

AT&T, 10

Autonetics, 9, 141, 164

Avistar Communications, 73

B

Bank of America, 73

Bristol, George, 133, 140

Boeing, 9

Bourns, 10, 17, 22, 72

Burnett, Jerry, 73

C

Carson, Johnny, 131

CCH (*also see Wolters Kluwer*), 142, 143, 165, 169

Christopher, Warren, 135

Chu, Dr. G.Y., 50

Clay, Don, 106

Cline, Pat, 42, 43, 44

Clinitec, 42, 43

Clinton, Bill, 135

Cohen, Morris, 37, 38

Coopers and Lybrand, 141

D

Data General Nova, 50

Dental Group Management Association (DGMA), 105

Diamond, Dan, 73

Digital Equipment Corporation, 50

Documate, 73, 74

Dreyfuss, Norman, 140

Dreyfuss, Richard, 140

E

Eastman Kodak, 50, 51

Edson de Castro, 50

Ellison, Larry, 13

Enron, 60

ePace!, 22, 142, 143, 165, 167, 169

Evans, Jean, 15

F

Facebook, 30

Federal Express (FedEx), 47, 48

Feldman, 6

Frehner, Graeme, 10, 13, 14, 15, 16, 21, 34, 35, 41, 84, 85, 89, 103, 104, 132, 133, 134, 140, 168

G

Gates, Bill, 33

Gerrity, Thomas, 73, 74

Gibson, Dunne, and Crutcher, 135

Google, 30, 31

Grove, Andy, 49

T

Tallahassee Ear Nose and Throat
(TNT), 44

Technology Bookstore, 7

Tesla, 69

Twitter, 30, 31

V

Vicor Inc, 73

Virgin Galactic, 119

Vogelpol, John, 10 ,72

W

Wall Street, 134, 164

Wang Computers, 50

Wang, Dr. An, 50

Weissman, Bruce, 104

Weissman, John, 104

Williams, Evan, 30

Williams, Ted, 29, 33

Wolters Kluwer (*also see CCH*), 142, 165

Wonderland Greyhound Park, 2

Wozniak, Steve, 33, 35

Wyle, David, 122, 141, 142, 143

Wyle, Henry, 141

Y

Yilunto, Carl, 22

Z

ZeroGravity, 119

Zuckerberg, Mark, 30